Reaching Families

PAUL BUTLER
Reaching Families

SCRIPTURE UNION
130 CITY ROAD LONDON EC1V 2NJ

© Paul Butler 1995

First published 1995

ISBN 0 86201 972 9

All rights reserved. No part of this publication may be reproduced, stored in a retrieval system, or transmitted, in any form or by any means, electronic, mechanical, photocopying, recording or otherwise, without the prior permission of Scripture Union.

The right of Paul Butler to be identified as author of this work has been asserted by him in accordance with the Copyright, Designs and Patents Act 1988.

Scriptures quoted from the *Good News Bible* published by The Bible Societies/Harper Collins Publishers Ltd., UK, © The American Bible Society, 1966, 1971, 1976, 1992.

British Library Cataloguing-in-Publication Data
A catalogue record for this book is available from the British Library.

Cover illustration and design by Mark Carpenter Design Consultants.

Phototypeset by Intype, London.

Printed and bound in Great Britain by Cox & Wyman Ltd., Reading.

This book is dedicated to the 'families' of St Paul's, East Ham and St Mary's with St Stephen's, Walthamstow.

CONTENTS

FOREWORD		9
INTRODUCTION		11
1	The family today	13
2	The family album	15
3	The family God	27
4	God in a family	41
5	God's family people	49
6	Family life opportunities	63
7	Parenting	81
8	Family support	91
9	Family to family	101
10	Getting away from it all	109
11	'One off' family events	123
12	The gospel that divides?	131
13	Families of the future	139

FOREWORD

I have been one of the 'lucky' ones; so has Rosemary, my wife. We have both grown up in happy, stable families. We have had good experiences not just of the nuclear family but of a much more extended kind of family too. I cannot remember a Christmas when I was growing up with less than thirteen people present and it was more often around twenty: and we all enjoyed it. We still do. I am deeply grateful to God and to all my relatives for these good experiences of family. They have meant a great deal to me. So thank you to my grandparents (all deceased), parents, sisters, aunts, uncles and cousins galore. You are all special people.

Yet I have met many people for whom family has been a far more painful experience. They have taught me about family in all kinds of ways. This book owes as much to them as it does to my immediate family.

'Family' has in fact become one of those rather slippery words that are difficult to define. That is why the book opens with a look at an outline theology of the family. What does God think about it all? And is 'family' a word that we can use to refer to those who claim allegiance to God in and through Jesus of Nazareth? We have to have some idea about these things if we are to know what we mean when we talk about 'reaching families' with the good news (gospel) of Jesus Christ. So I hope that you will not skip straight to the chapters which appear to be about the 'how to': they will make less sense without an

Foreword

understanding of the thinking that underlies the practice. Yet at the end of the day this book is about practice. We need to be reaching out to families with God's good news: heaven knows they need it! When you are ready to get on with the task perhaps you will want to use some of the ideas included in this book; perhaps you have your own. I don't pretend to have all the answers and indeed I am deeply suspicious of anyone who tries to suggest that they do! I believe that there are a multiplicity of ways of working with families because every family is different and God is big enough to meet with each one as they need to be met.

As ever, no book is simply the product of one person. I am deeply grateful once again to Rosemary, Caroline, David, Andrew and Sarah for their love and patience as I have taken time out to write. I am also grateful for the encouragement of Janet Morgan and Joan King in keeping me at it. Alison Barr's editorial patience and sharpness have been superb (you're a gem). The friendship and support of all my colleagues at Scripture Union over seven years, especially those in the Missions Department, have been magnificent and to them I owe many of the ideas contained within the following pages. Sarah, you have been a brilliant co-worker: keep developing.

As a family we are also deeply thankful to the people of Walthamstow for welcoming the strangers in so quickly and warmly. We look forward to years of 'family ministry' with you. But in this instance my biggest debt is to the 'family' of St Paul's, East Ham: for all you have been to us over the past six years – a huge thank you. You have taught us more than we could ever say.

INTRODUCTION

It was Father's Day, that great festival invented by the card manufacturers. As a family we were away together. I was speaking and leading sessions at a church family weekend on the theme of 'Being God's People Together'. People of all ages were there. Just before breakfast our three eldest children came into the bedroom. They presented me with a pile of wonderfully handmade and designed cards (one in the eye for the card manufacturers). They were terrific. Inside Caroline's card was sellotaped a little red square. Inside this little envelope was a tiny book she had made. The cover read 'Reaching Families'. On the next page it read 'Chapter One: Adults care for the children' and over the page, 'Chapter Two: Children care for the adults'.

I was coming towards the end of writing this book at the time and it had featured large in the life of the whole family. Caroline's delightful little act spoke volumes to me. She had summed up the heart of what reaching anyone is about: caring. Love is what reaches people and love is seen by the way we care. Yet she had done more than that. She had not written 'Parents care for your children' or 'Children care for your parents'. At nearly nine, she understood that many more adults are involved in the life of a child than just the parents. Grandparents, aunts, uncles, neighbours and friends all come into the picture too. Family life for Caroline is far broader than simply the six of us who share our home together; though we are a central part of it. Equally vital for her, and for the rest of

Introduction

us, is God. The Creator is at the heart of family. The Creator cares: for adults and for children without distinction.

What follows in the book are ideas and suggestions as to how God's loving care might be communicated to families today. But at the outset let this younger member of the Butler family summarise the heart of it: 'care'.

1
THE FAMILY TODAY

Walking down my local high street I can see many different family groups going from shop to shop: families that consist of two parents and a number of children; single-parent-families; older couples who may, or may not, have grown up children living elsewhere; couples seemingly without children; and people on their own. They come from a wide range of racial, social and cultural backgrounds. As I watch them looking at things they often cannot afford, clamouring either out loud (usually the children) or quietly inside for the latest fashion in music, clothes, toys, videos or whatever, I can imagine what kind of pressures and strains they may be feeling in life and in their family: emotional pressures, financial strains, awkwardness in relating to one another. But it's also easy to imagine lots of joys: laughter, the delight in giving to each other, the fun at being together and discovering more about each other's likes and dislikes, the sheer enjoyment in being family.

Then I notice that in the midst of the crowds in the high street there are families from the church family to which I belong. They too are from a wide range of family types and they are experiencing the same joys and pressures in being family as everyone else.

Yet I know that there is something different about these Christians in families. They have discovered that God loves them and is concerned for them and their lives. They know that the Good News of Jesus Christ is true and are beginning to live in the experience of that, however tentatively, by the power of the Holy Spirit. So they are the same, yet they are different. And I long that the first families I observed may become families who are different and yet the same as well. I want to reach them. I want them to know God's love for them in all its glorious fulness. But how?

The key for me lies in the very two factors I have described: the *similarity* between Christians in families and those who are not Christians in families – the joys, difficulties, pains and achievements that are common to each; and the *difference* between Christians in families and those who are not Christians in families – in their membership of the one great family of God.

It is through these two factors that we will discover ways of reaching out to families with the love of God. It is primarily by being family that families will be reached. And it is by being God's family together, that we will be able to reach families who as yet have not discovered the difference that being in that family makes.

2

THE FAMILY ALBUM

In our home we have a vast array of photograph albums, testimony to the ubiquitous nature of the camera in the modern world. We also have a small number of photographs going back to the last century when the whole art of photography was far more complex and expensive. All the old photographs are of family members from the past. Some are individual photos, others are family groups. Many of the modern photos are also of family members, usually in rather less formal poses; they act as a record of the children's growth, and the ageing of parents, grandparents, aunts, uncles, and friends. They evoke memories of holidays and family gatherings. Sometimes they provoke laughter and animated conversation; sometimes tears as memories of a beloved family member come flooding back.

Our family albums tell us something about the nature and make-up of our family, and something of its history. They create an interesting problem of definition. Who makes up our family?

At one level, for us, it is husband, wife and four children living under the same roof. But at another level, it is grandparents, aunts, uncles, cousins, great uncles, great aunts, second cousins, third cousins, sisters- and brothers-in-law and so on. (It also depends a little on who is doing the defining of course; an uncle who is very important to me is quite possibly a very distant figure to my children or a complete unknown to my brothers-in-law.) Furthermore, we do not regard the living family as the family in its entirety. Rosemary's father died several years ago but he is still a part of us; his influence lives on, the memories remain; the longing that he had known our two younger children and the feeling that he would have loved to see all four of them growing up only partially diminish with time. Within this family there are married couples with children and without; single people (unmarried, separated, divorced or widowed); children, teenagers, young adults, middle-aged adults and both early and late elderly.

Family is thus, for us, all-aged and extended rather than the tight nuclear family, though the latter features as an important element throughout the extended one.

But this is simply our family. Others would have a different pattern. The single person who has never married may well see brothers, sisters, nephews and nieces, for example, in a rather different light from the way we see them. The person who has been divorced and re-married and has children from both marriages may well find defining a family tree or map rather more complicated. For someone who is an only child of parents who were also both lone children, the whole family tree is very much smaller. Or take this interesting account from Barbara Ehrenreich:

> 'My son's recent graduation from college was attended by nearly fifty of his closest relatives and their current significant others. We are talking about parents and step-parents, grandparents and step-grandparents, ex-step-parents and the children they have acquired in subsequent marriages, plus nubile young siblings clutching the hands of their future ex-spouses.'
>
> (*The Guardian* 11 November 1994)

The family album

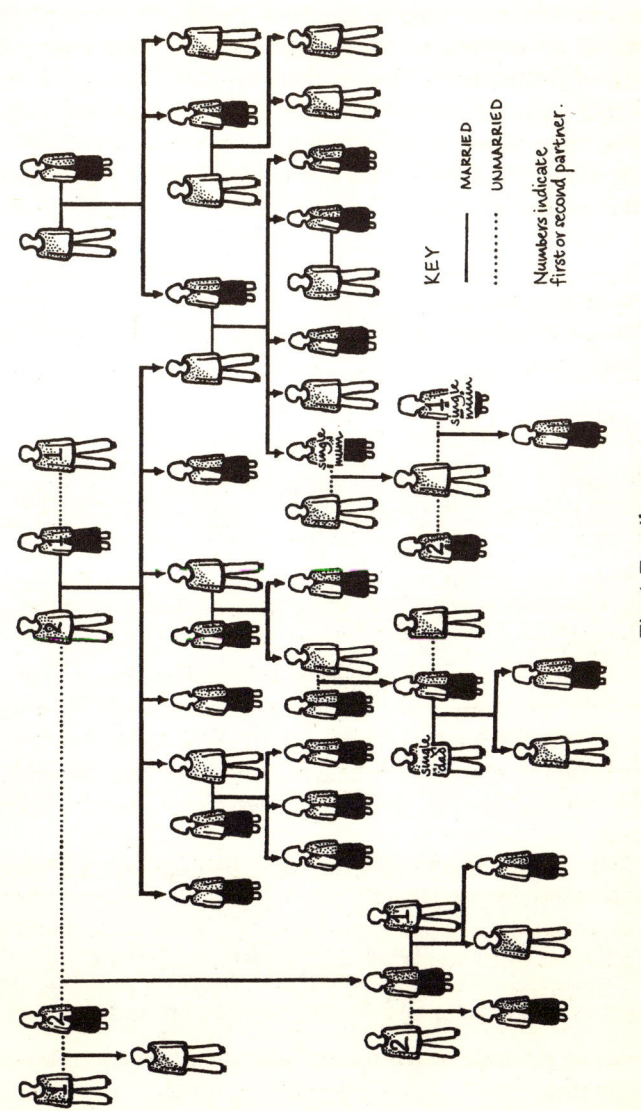

Fig 1 Family tree

This, however, is simply to define family by connecting lines of relationship. We all know that relationship is rather different from this. To be real, it is about how we actually live in connection with each other. What communication takes place? How do we value each other? How do we express that valuing and love? How do we handle our disagreements, likes and dislikes? And how do we cope together with the need everyone has for both personal space and companionship? To illustrate this let's close our family album for now and instead take a video camera with us and catch some images of 'family' in action around us.

Family Video Diary
The camera first picks up a father and son working together on a car: mother is probably in the house, but all the rest of the nuclear part of this family have grown up and moved away. As we watch, the daughter, son-in-law and first grandchild arrive for a visit. The work on the car stops as greetings are exchanged then recommences as the new arrivals go inside the house.

Next the camera picks up an elderly widow living alone. Family is very important to her: she has five children all living away from home now. There are grandchildren who visit regularly and there's the friend over the road who has been a friend for life, who also lives alone and feels like family.

Then there follows a series of video 'shorts' all shot within a brief time span:

Parents weep at the funeral of their child; so many dreams shattered, not just for them but for the grandparents, the brothers and sisters, and the community around them all.

Smiles of pleasure at the cricket ground as proud children watch their father score the winning runs in the village cup; parents-in-law, spouse, sister- and brother-in-law are

The family album

cheering their hearts out as the village hail their local hero.

A father hugs his children with tears rolling down his cheeks as he tells them that Mummy will never be coming home again: she has died in hospital of cancer.

Forty people gather together to celebrate a ruby wedding: child, daughter-in-law, grandchildren, aged aunt, cousins, friends and neighbours all enjoy the party.

A single mum and her child share and laugh together as they recount the excitement of a weekend away with friends at Granny and Grandpa's.

Men and boys gather outside a beautifully decorated house: they are all smartly dressed. Around the corner, women and girls surround another equally beautifully decorated house as they wait for the bride to appear from within. The family have come from all corners of the nation and the world to celebrate this happy wedding week in true Sikh fashion.

A widow is escorted by her single son, her only child, as they join with hundreds from the community to celebrate the new church buildings being opened.

Men and women celebrate the life of their friend: the parents feel on the edge of it all because they could never quite come to terms with their son's sexual orientation. The sense of 'family' between the 'gay' friends is, however, a revelation to them. AIDS has created a loving bond that is rare in any other community.

A single woman, who has always wanted to marry and have children but never met 'the right man', consoles her married brothers and sisters and mother whom her father appears to be mistreating after fifty years of marriage.

A mother desperately missing her children whilst she is

away from home in a strange country on business: her children are with grandparents and friends because her husband is also away on business. She is welcomed into a home and enjoys the life of another family in another culture.

All of these video pictures are real, drawn simply from snapshots in time of my own 'family' life. Joy, pain, pleasure, sorrow, questioning, changes, hopes, dreams, nightmares all feature as part of this family's life. The snapshots are also all, bar the opening two, quite dramatic and illustrate key moments. Day to day reality would usually be edited out of the video because it was too mundane and boring – a lot of footage about sleeping, washing, shopping, eating and particular everyday activities of family members like school, playgroup, work, pub, watching TV or videos, playing with the latest computer games and so forth. Yet this mundane footage would actually reveal a great deal of the truth about how family members really do function together.

Take eating, for example. In some homes eating is generally done together around the table or in front of the TV (or both); in others, eating together is a real rarity: individual members eat when they want to, usually in front of the TV or in their own room. Conversation over the meal, if it occurs at all, is likely to be limited to 'Pass the salt', 'Where's the ketchup?', and 'Oh by the way Mum, I'm going out tonight and I'll be back late'. The last may create a response, even an argument, but that will be that. There is very little real relating together, or sharing of what each other has been doing that day.

Surveys reveal how little actual communication takes place between family members, especially between fathers and their children. On average most adults only spend a few minutes each week talking to, at or with their children. It is quite likely that one family member may spend more

The family album

time in real conversation and communication with a parent or sibling living at a distance than with the members of the family in the same household. The telephone makes this not only possible but commonplace in some families' lives.

> **Stop**
> Reflect on some stories of your own that give you images of family life.

Family Facts
The family album and family video diary are about impressions and images. They create false impressions just as the camera can tell lies. The photo of the happy smiling nuclear family can hide abuse, arguments and divisions very easily. The editor's razor sharp knife can remove all the unpleasant scenes that have been recorded or it can accentuate the importance of these by removing all the joy and happiness. So it is also valuable to have some hard facts and figures about family life. These need to be not simply about numbers in families, though these are important, but also about social patterns, finances and expectations, if they are to create a real picture of family life today. So let's put some of the facts and figures down. The figures quoted are all for the United Kingdom unless otherwise stated, and drawn mainly from the work of the Family Policy Studies Centre and the European Value Systems Study Group.

Children in Families
98% of children live with their natural mother.

Nearly 70% of children are born to couples in their first marriage.

32% of children are now born 'outside marriage' but half of these are born to couples who are cohabiting.

The average number of children in a 'family' is 1.9.

Marriage and Cohabiting

The average age for first marriages is rising – it is twenty-four at present.

81% of people marry by the time they are fifty.

The average length of a marriage is ten to eleven years (it was fifteen in Victorian England when most marriages ended with the death of a partner).

57% of divorced people re-marry within 5 years, often after a period of cohabitation.

Cohabiting as an option is increasingly popular. A majority of couples cohabit before marriage. Some would cite finance as a major reason for this option (for example, they are saving to be able to afford a big wedding and smart honeymoon).

40% of marriages end in divorce. Second and subsequent marriages are more likely to end in divorce than first marriages especially when children from the previous marriage(s) form part of the reconstituted family.

Some cohabiting couples are of the same sex and some of these have children.

Singleness

33% of all households are lone person households.

67% of these households consist of retired people. Many more of these are women than men, largely due to the longer lifespan of women.

The family album

Employment Patterns
Only 16% of households are made up of a husband at work with the wife at home caring for children.

Large numbers of mothers who are employed only work part time.

Lone mothers are less likely to be employed than married or cohabiting mothers.

The pressures created by unemployment (mainly financial and devaluation of self-esteem) are often involved in creating disturbance and break up in family life.

Extended Family
Greater mobility and the need to move to find work mean that the pattern of families all living in the same street or neighbourhood throughout their lives has become increasingly less common.

However, telephones, cassette recorders, video cameras and the ease of travel all mean that communication between family members often remains high. Family visits and help at particular times of need (eg birth of a baby, death of a partner, sickness) remain very common and strong. The extended family has changed its form but it has certainly not disappeared.

On the other hand the number of people who have no immediate family to offer this kind of care and support, particularly in old age, is high and places great demands on both the state and voluntary welfare agencies.

Stop
Take time to look back over these facts and figures.

- What are your reactions and feelings about them?

- Do any in particular encourage you? Frighten you? Worry you? Why?
- What can you do to work out these reactions and feelings?

The 3D Family Picture

Using the impressions and images gained from our family albums and video diaries, alongside the rather more clinical facts and figures we have considered, we can begin to draw several conclusions about families and family life today.

1 Families are very diverse in nature. You can define a family as husband, wife and two children if you want to, but such a definition is far too narrow to reflect reality; most of the population of the UK, and indeed, of the whole world do not live in such families. We have, rather, to be prepared to draw a whole range of family models that extend beyond a nuclear core which is itself diverse in its nature.

2 Families are enormously important to people of all ages, backgrounds, lifestyles and beliefs. To deny this is to deny a fundamental reality of life worldwide. For all the conflicts and pain that occur within families, they are also the key source of friendship and support for most people. You only have to stop all those people in the high street and ask them which group of people is most important to them, and they will nine times out of ten say 'family'.

3 Families are places of great joy, and great pain. They are regularly the central sources of love and value for people, but they are also regularly sources of great bitterness and anguish. To depict family life as all sweetness and light is like painting over a patch of mould on a wall and pretending that the mould is not there. Before

The family album

long it will show through again. But equally families are often where the mould is cleared away and treated.

4 Everyone's life is, to a large extent, shaped by the family around them. John Donne wrote, 'No man is an island, entire of itself', and he was right. We ignore the family context of anyone at our peril. Working with an individual as an island is bound to limit our understanding and the quality of help we will be able give. Western society has become highly individualistic but the family nature of every human being is inherent and will reveal itself somewhere along the way.

5 Changing patterns in parenting, cohabiting, divorce and re-marriage, work, economic conditions and the ageing population will inevitably have an impact on family life.

This dynamic picture of family, full as it is of joys and hopes as well as pressures and pains, encompasses all families regardless of whether or not they have members who are Christian believers. Christians in families experience all the same joys and all the same pressures as everyone else. It may be the case that fewer instances of divorce happen in families which have Christians in them, but divorce certainly still happens in such families. There are Christians who are lone parents – single, cohabiting, re-marrying – facing financial strain, encountering health problems, unemployment, and relationship breakdown with children and other family members. We need to be honest about this and face the reality of the similarity of the lives of Christians in families with the lives of everyone else.

Throughout the book we will seek to keep before us the realities of family life for all people, and work with these rather than operate from an ideal which does not exist and never has existed. In other words we will work from the basis that families are made up of imperfect human beings. As we work with the reality of family in our world forgiveness, compassion and understanding will be crucial to all that we do.

Stop

Think of one 'family' from your own earlier reflections who are not part of a church family.

- How do you think it would help with the task of introducing them to God's love and family, to work with them as they actually are, rather than expecting them to conform to a particular image of what 'family' should be?

- What might be the dangers of this approach?

- Having thought this through for one family, think more broadly. What might be the advantages of working from the position of 'the family as it actually is', for reaching families in general outside of the church?

- What might be the dangers of this approach?

For Further Reading
Trends in Britain, ed Martyn Eden, Monarch, 1933 (especially the chapter on 'Family' by Joan King).

The Family Policy Studies Centre publishes several reports on family life in Britain generally. Contact them at 231 Baker Street, London NW1; telephone 0171–486 7680.

Restructuring Family Values, Anne Borrowdale, SPCK, 1994.

3

THE FAMILY GOD

Family is God's idea and God's intention. The truth is that the Creator of all things is 'the family God'. Not in some nice, cosy domestic sense, but rather in the very dynamic of God's being and the creative nature of that which he has made. In order to think clearly about the nature of families and the task of reaching out to them with the love of their creator, we need to explore this further.

Three in One and One in Three

> Three in one, yet one in three.
> God the Holy Trinity.
> Nice for theologians,
> But nought to do with me.

The doctrine of the Trinity has so often been presented as a theological mystery that large numbers of Christians have thought it largely the domain of the theological debaters and irrelevant to their daily lives. This is a tragedy.

The very fact that so much energy was spent in the early centuries of Christendom arguing over, developing and defending the doctrine, indicates that there was far more at stake than simply theological niceties. The debate was about the very nature and being of God and of how he has made himself known in and to the created order.

Understanding something of God's being enables us to understand something of our own and of our purpose. If we have got God wrong, then everything else is going to be distorted (*cf* Isaiah 40; Job 38–41).

The heart of the conviction that God is three persons within the one Godhead is that God is in himself 'family' or 'community', and entirely complete as such. In whatever way we seek to picture the existence of God as three in one, we have to come up with images of mutuality and unity. One can use, as an example, Augustine's classic image of God as love: he is the lover (the Father); the beloved (the Son); and the love which flows back and forth between these two (the Holy Spirit). Here is love in perfection (*cf* Romans 5; 1 John 4:7–21).

The very language which is used to describe God in the three persons is language drawn from 'family': Father (eg Matthew 6:8–15; Galatians 4:6) and Son (Matthew 3:17; Hebrews 1). Whilst 'Spirit' is less obviously drawn from this sphere, descriptions of the Spirit as the Counsellor (NIV, John 14:16, 26; some versions have the Comforter or the Helper) and as the Spirit of sonship (Romans 8:14–17; Galatians 4:6–7) reveal the family nature of the Spirit's character and work.

Inevitably there is a problem for us in exploring this further. We are seeking to enter into and grasp something of the inner life of the Almighty, and by definition the Almighty is way beyond the individual or collective grasp of small, weak, finite human beings. However there is enough here to tell us that God in himself exists as a divine community, made up of distinct persons, yet in total mutuality, operating as one God. One description which has always gripped me is that of the Trinity as an eternal dance: Father, Son and Spirit constantly, and in perfection, interweaving, cooperating, appreciating, glorifying and upholding each other in one complex dance.

At this point I imagine readers dividing into two groups.

The family God

Some will be deeply concerned about the apparent maleness of all this imagery whilst others will be saying: 'I was right all along; it is just for theologians. How does this affect my daily life?' To the first group, I apologise and refer them to the extended note on God as Father and Mother at the end of this chapter; then please return and read on. To those who are only troubled by the second question, please keep going.

> **Stop**
>
> Take time to reflect on the above. Decide whether or not you want to reflect on God as Mother as well as Father. If so turn to the end of the chapter. If not, reflect on God as God in community.

Made in the Image of the Family God

The opening chapter of the Bible makes it abundantly clear that God is the Creator of all things. Yet within this creativity a special place and purpose is given to humankind. Human beings were made 'in the likeness or image of God'. Now if God is love and is a community within himself, then that community likeness of God must be included within the human make-up. Humankind is made for relationship, community and family because that is part of what the likeness of God is all about (Genesis 1:26–31). This community reflection of God comes across in the fact that God made human beings, male and female, to live and work together to care for the created order.

This deeply social nature of being human becomes apparent in the account of the making of man (Adam), the naming of the animals, and the making of woman (Eve) (Genesis 2). There is a social interaction between man and the animal kingdom, which we ignore to our detriment. But there is a deeper, fuller interaction within humanity between man and woman. It seems that something of the outworking of the divine image requires both male and female and social relationship between them.

This account goes further, however, and tells us that the union of a man and a woman in a committed covenant relationship is foundational to how God's purposes will be worked out in God's world. Marriage, not here as legal status but as covenant relationship made within the broader social context, is seen as a divine ordinance built into the very fabric of creation. It appears that it was always God's intention that the fulfilling of the call to multiply and fill the earth was to be done in and through the context of such covenant relationships; thus family units were anticipated from the outset. The creation of 'family' as a unit within the broader human family was thus established at the very beginning of the Bible because it reflects the very character of God to the world that he has made. Jesus endorsed the creation nature of marriage (Matthew 19:4–6) and the divine intention contained within this.

It follows from this that in one sense the whole human race can be seen as one human family intended to enjoy the overflowing love of God and meant to reflect the family image of God in itself to the rest of the creation. It also follows that in one sense every smaller family unit within this one human family draws its very existence and name from God himself; an idea which Paul seems to be communicating in Ephesians 3:14–15.

Yet, whilst the ideal of the Creator stands firm, the nature of the created order has become seriously disrupted and defective.

Family Breakdown

From the instant that man and woman chose to think that they knew better than their Maker, breakdown in

The family God

relationship entered human experience. The decision to act self-centredly, rather than God-centredly, established a rift in every area of relationship that God had made. The open relationship with God was broken, the mutuality between man and woman was ruptured and the harmonious relationship between humanity and the created order was lost (Genesis 3). This disruption of relationship and community spilled over into the family structure very rapidly as the story of Cain and Abel graphically illustrates. From this point on the Bible continually depicts family relationships as less than ideal. Take, for example, the status and treatment of Hagar and Ishmael within Abraham's extended family (Genesis 16 and 21); or Jacob's double dealing with his brother Esau and father Isaac, only to be followed later by the incredible favouritism he showed towards Joseph and his over-protectiveness of Benjamin (Genesis 27, 37, 42). In fact on no occasion is any family depicted as without fault or failure, not even that of Jesus himself (see the disbelief and apparent scheming of his brothers in John 7:1ff).

Yet God worked in grace in and through these broken, severely messed up families to bring about his ultimate purposes. So he used Jacob's scheming, jealousy and protectiveness. The Judaic line which would eventually lead to the birth of the Messiah began with Judah mistaking his daughter-in-law, Tamar, for a prostitute and fathering twins by her (Genesis 38). When David committed adultery with Bathsheba and had Uriah killed, God rebuked him and punished him through the death of the child, but did not remove him from the throne or punish Bathsheba (2 Samuel 11, 12); rather, their second child, Solomon, became the next king. Throughout the Old Testament God worked in and through families in which polygamy, adultery, abuse and power politics all took place. The genealogy of Matthew is interesting for its mention of only four women other than Mary: Tamar (whose situation we noted above); Rahab, a prostitute; Ruth, a foreigner; and Bathsheba (Matthew 1:3–6). This certainly does not mean God condones adultery or evil but it does show that his grace works through all kinds of events and all kinds of families.

Grace, redemption, renewal and fresh starts are available for all it seems. Hence, I want to suggest, the Bible itself effectively urges us to work with families as they are in reality rather than as we might want them to be. Yet it calls us to do this without ever losing sight of the divine origin and place of the family. And further, it offers God-given laws within which family life should operate so far as possible, and outside of which problems will inevitably arise.

Family Law and Structure

The whole of Jewish society was structured carefully. Individuals belonged to Israel, the people of God. But each individual was part of a family. The family name was important, so important that every effort was to be made to maintain it down through the generations (Deuteronomy 25:5–6; Ruth 4; Matthew 22:24). Each family was then part of a larger related group, the clan. Several clans together made up a tribe which could trace its history back to one of Jacob's sons. Then together the twelve tribes made up the whole people of Israel, descended from Jacob, Isaac and Abraham to whom God had made his covenant promises. They were thus together constituted as the people of God by their direct lineage from Abraham, Isaac and Jacob, but also because they were the people of promise, the people of the covenant. The reason for the genealogies throughout the Old Testament is to establish and maintain these family ties; they are not mere lists but vital to maintaining each tribe's, clan's, family's and individual's identity (see Numbers 1–4; Joshua 13–22; 1 Chronicles 1–9; Matthew 1).

The family God

This overall structure clearly meant that the family was always regarded as an extended group. It was never confined in Israel to husband, wife and their own children. The marriage relationship was key, as the strong prohibition on adultery makes clear, but it did not create a new exclusive family group. Physically families lived together in an extended fashion. Marriages were arranged within the extended family group or within the clan, though there were tight rules about not marrying someone too closely related either by blood or marriage (Leviticus 18).

Nevertheless within this extended family there were key roles given to parents and responsibilities placed upon them and their children. Education, in particular spiritual teaching, was largely the role of both parents (Deuteronomy 6, 11; Proverbs 1–7). Providing for the well-being of the children was in the hands of the parents, though employers and the wider society had to make sure that they did nothing to hinder that provision and they were to offer support when it was failing. Children had a duty to honour and respect their parents throughout their years. The fourth commandment was given to all of Israel and had no age limits placed on it. How the honour was given no doubt changed as children grew older. In later life it certainly meant caring for elderly and weak parents. It also meant that the wisdom of the aged was respected and valued.

Then when the system of care within the family broke down, the wider family and society had no option but to take on the responsibility. So children who were left without a father (or father and mother) were to be provided for, as were women left without a husband. People coming from outside Israel were also to be welcomed and their needs supplied. Failure to provide in this way was strongly condemned by the prophets.

This was a very different society from that of the modern

Western world. But through the Old Testament period Jewish society changed as it moved from a nomadic existence to a settled one; from a loose tribal confederation into a centrally ruled monarchy; as iron replaced bronze; as it adapted to life in exile, and reflected on how to live on return from exile. Yet through all these changes family and the extended nature of family remained important. The determination with which his people ensured that the vulnerable were particularly cared for showed how true to God's character they were actually being. Family was always on the agenda.

Conclusions

The importance of all of this to the church seeking to reach families with the good news is clear.

1 Family, living in families, is God's idea and is built into the very fabric of creation. So a concern *solely* with the salvation of individuals is inadequate. We are called to help families understand something of the divine purpose in family life. We should want to see families who are tied together by blood and covenant, also tied together by their faith in God and their belonging together to the people of God.

2 Families are always affected by human brokenness. So, whilst there are ideals and guidelines, we need to be realistic about this brokenness.

3 God is the God of grace who works in and through broken families and convoluted human relationships. So we should expect him to be the same for our own family and for those we are trying to reach.

4 Family is meant to be a place of care and provision. So we need to help it to be that for all its members whatever their status or age.

The family God

5 Family has always been part of an extended group of people, related by blood and covenant within a wider community. So we should work with this broad community base as well as individuals and smaller family units if we really want to work for the well-being of all.

This all sounds like a highly demanding task. It is. But this is not the full picture. For God is not the 'family' God only because it is essential to his own being and existence, expressed outwardly through and in his creation. He is also the 'family' God because he is the one who has humbled himself, left heaven and actually lived on earth as a family person. He is the God who has lived in a family.

Stop

Consider the ideal of the whole human family acting as one family.

- What would the glorious possibilities of this be?
- Consider the place of smaller family units within this greater family. What is their value and role?
- Consider a Bible family such as Abraham's or Jacob's. What caused some of the breakdowns to occur?

Extended Note on God as Father and Mother

The Jews had become used to calling God 'Father' by the time of Jesus, though it is a rare title for God in the Old Testament. Where it is used in the Old Testament, it refers to the relationship between God and Israel as a people (Exodus 4:22; Deuteronomy 32:6; Isaiah 63:16 and 64:8; Jeremiah 3:4,19). There was no real concept of God as Father of individuals except in the relationship of God to the Messiah (2 Samuel 7:14; Psalm 89:26; Isaiah 9:6). It was thus as 'Father of Israel' that the term was in use in Jesus' own day.

He, however, apparently revolutionised the use of this title for God. In referring frequently to God as his own Father, he was claiming the messianic relationship for himself (this is particularly strong in John's Gospel, eg John 2:16; 5:17ff; 8:17ff, but see also the Synoptic Gospels, eg Matthew 11:27; Mark 14:36; Luke 23:34, 46). He also broadened and deepened the meaning of the title. His use of the more intimate and personal *Abba* implied a greater individuality and personal depth to this relationship.

But Jesus went further than this and taught his disciples that their relationship with God could also be seen in terms of calling God 'Father', expressing the intimacy of the relationship between God and his people which the Messiah would bring about through the new covenant (Matthew 6:5–15; Luke 11:1–13; John 20:17). This was clearly also the emphasis in the teaching of the early church. A new intimacy of relationship had come about through the death, resurrection and glorification of Jesus and the coming of the Holy Spirit into the lives of those who acknowledged him to be both Lord and Christ (Romans 8:15; Galatians 4:6; 1 Peter 1:17–21; 1 John 3:1).

The intention of all of this is not to create the impression that God is male, nor even that the relationship between God and his people is akin to that of a father with his children rather than that of a mother with hers. It is rather to give God a name and title of intimacy and affection, whilst also acknowledging his greatness and authority.

Indeed both Old and New Testaments are not scared to liken God's attitude towards his people with that of a mother towards her children. In some instances these similes are not even those of a human mother but of motherly actions in the natural world. Note for example the mother

The family God

eagle image of Deuteronomy 32:10, 11; or Jesus' use of the mother hen (Luke 13:34). God likens himself to a breastfeeding mother who 'has borne' her children (Isaiah 49:15); she is the one who feeds them and teaches them to walk (Hosea 11) – both activities more associated with the mother than the father in Jewish households. Indeed the whole ethos of God caring for his people as little children tends to equate God's activity with that of the mother rather than the father, as Paul himself indicates when describing his own pastoral care of the young Thessalonican Christians (1 Thessalonians 2:7).

Hence God's 'fatherly' care encompasses the total parental care offered by the combination of father and mother, male and female. We need to take care that we communicate this overall 'parent' role of God to people whenever we talk of God as Father or Mother.

So, given the changed nature of our own Western culture and the common understanding of the word 'father' within this culture, should we start calling God 'Mother' or 'Mother and Father' or 'Parent'? For myself I have a great deal of sympathy with those who want to make some such change but cannot quite bring myself to going along with it wholeheartedly.

I even question whether it is purely a problem of modern Western cultural understanding. Is not the importance of the Virgin Mary in Christian history partly to do with the longing for a motherly figure at the heart of God? And what of the testimony to the motherliness of God found in the medieval writings of people like Julian of Norwich? Is it not more deeply and fundamentally to do with the cry from within all humanity for the loving care that is encompassed only fully in the maternal and paternal qualities expressed in the male and female? This ought to be expected because, in making humankind in his own image, God made male and female. There was something lacking when only the male form was around.

So given this, what conclusions do I reach? I have no problem with referring to God as 'Heavenly Parent' on occasions, if for no other reason than to avoid unnecessary offence to those who find 'father' such a difficult term because of their experience of human fathers. I can also happily refer to God as 'Motherly Father' and I am open to persuasion on the occasional use even of 'Father and Mother of us all'. But I cannot move to referring simply to God as 'Mother' for two main reasons. First it seems to me that there is no scriptural warrant for referring to God by this title alone, despite the willingness of scripture to use motherly imagery. Second, it seems to me that we are followers of our Lord who taught his disciples to call God, 'Father'.

This intimacy of address was clearly adequate for Jesus' own communion with the One with whom he had spent eternity. Jesus was not afraid to upset theological apple carts by using ideas and terms which were not acceptable to the religious authorities of his day, so I see no reason why he could not have chosen to refer to God as 'Mother' if he had seen it as appropriate. The fact that, so far as scripture tells us, he did not, cannot be set aside lightly. I am prepared to settle for the simplicity of, 'If "Father" was good enough for the Lord, then it is good enough for me' – so long as I am continually open to discovering new depths within the motherly fatherhood of God, and constantly recognise that we need to rescue 'Father' from the very male, rather distant and domineering meaning that it has had built into it in Western culture over the centuries.

One further thought. Great pains have been taken in theological works on the Holy Spirit to uphold and maintain the personality of the Spirit. Great play is made of the use of the personal pronoun with the normally neutral Spirit in the New Testament. This is important, but could not the work of the Spirit be seen in more 'motherly' terms? After all, is not the description of the fruit of the Spirit in Galatians 5:22 full of terms often used to describe the female? Care needs to be taken here because it would certainly be wrong to try and depict the Father as 'male' and the Spirit as 'female', but it seems to me that it would help us grasp more fully the motherly nature of 'Father', if we could meditate on the work of the Spirit who is described, for example, as bringing us to new birth (John 3:5–8).

I know that some readers will feel I have gone too far in these lines of argument, whilst others will accuse me of lacking the courage to go the whole way. I hope both will respect the position that I have propounded here and which I know is held by many others. It is not simply a *via media*: it is held after much careful thought, in all honesty before the Creator.

4

GOD IN A FAMILY

Being the originator of 'family', it is hardly surprising that scripture contains instructions from God about how to live as families. Yet this is not the whole story: the more wondrous fact is that God entered into this world as a human being and lived out his life in a family in Nazareth amongst other families spread across Galilee.

Jesus: God in a Family
Both Joseph and Mary were members of families: their genealogies tell us this, as do the various details which come to light in the birth accounts of Matthew 1–2 and Luke 1–2. We cannot create a detailed sketch of these families, but that they were real and important is beyond dispute, and their make-up and membership would have influenced the life of Jesus himself.

Jesus, then, grew up within a family context. He had two parents, four brothers and some sisters (Matthew 13:55, 56). The family life centred around the carpentry business which Joseph ran and into which Jesus himself entered, probably along with his younger brothers and maybe his grandfather too. In such a business there would have been plenty of contact with the local community: liaising with other tradesmen over their needs for ploughs, carts, furniture and tools; helping to build people's homes, and probably being commandeered by the Romans to do work for them some times.

Family life would also have featured regular Sabbath worship at the synagogue along with the other Jews in Nazareth. Worship then included the celebration of the great Jewish festivals of Passover and Tabernacles, the Day of Atonement, plus daily prayers and worship in the home. There seems little doubt that the instructions of Deuteronomy 6 would have been diligently carried out within this home.

From the age of six Jesus would almost certainly have attended the synagogue every day to learn the Law and the Prophets and also how to read and write. This probably involved learning fresh languages. In adulthood Jesus normally spoke in Aramaic but clearly had a good grasp of the Hebrew scriptures. Given the existence of Greek versions of the Old Testament and the use of Latin by the Romans, he may even have had some knowledge of these two languages as well, though not from the synagogue school.

Life in a community the size of Nazareth would have been highly corporate: other family members and friends would have taken their share of caring for the boy Jesus and he would have valued their companionship. The reality and depth of this community life comes over clearly from the incident when Jesus was twelve recorded by Luke. Mary and Joseph were not being negligent to travel a day's journey assuming their eldest son to be amongst the company; it would have been common practice (Luke 2:41–52).

I am quite sure that as Jesus grew older, Mary and Joseph shared the stories surrounding his birth and that of his cousin John. But he would also have heard, from the wider community, stories of the Roman atrocities at nearby Sepphoris where 2000 Jews were killed all in one day; conversation about the locally garrisoned Romans, the exploits of the Zealots living out in the hills, the antics of the local tax collectors and much else besides. Nazareth was not an exclusively Jewish community. Roman soldiers worshipped Caesar and other Roman gods. Peoples of other ethnic groups living in the area had their own worship practices. Jesus developed as a Jew in something of a pluralistic community. His personal growth and development in all respects were shaped by his family and by his community.

Over the thirty years that passed before Jesus began his public ministry he would have shared in family bereavements (quite probably Joseph died during Jesus' teenage years) and in other tragedies; he would have known the impact of illness on family life. He probably experienced some of the economic ups and downs through which families go. He may well have had to shoulder the responsibility of being the family's main bread winner. Then in his public ministry he experienced further family pressures and tensions, including rejection by his own brothers, apparent doubts from his mother and the loss of his highly supportive, though very eccentric, cousin. He saw the tragedy of a widow losing her only son at Nain; the unusual household of only two sisters, Mary and Martha, and their brother, Lazarus, at Bethany; the specially constituted family of a leper community; the homes of his disciples.

In all of this, contrary to the traditions and norms of the day and the society, he remained single. He expressed a conviction that this was his calling for the sake of his work for his Father's kingdom. He demonstrated that to be a complete human being you do not have to marry. Singleness is an entirely valid, godly lifestyle and is of value to both family and community (Matthew 19:10, 11). As a single person, he also created a broad-based family for himself among his disciples. Here was a community committed to each other made up of those who were married, and those who were single; those who were wealthy and those who were not; the politically aware and the politically not bothered; male and female. This 'alternative' family was important for Jesus; it demonstrated something of what he knew God's people should be like, but it also gave him the 'family' companionship and support that he needed as both fully God and man.

So by his thorough involvement in his own kinship family life and the family life of a committed community he demonstrated that all human beings belong in families and need families. Right up until his death he was concerned for his mother and for her 'family' life, and for the 'family' needs of his disciples. His practical concern for them backs up his teaching on the centrality of 'family'.

Jesus: Teaching about Family

Jesus clearly taught that in creation God intended the covenant relationship of a man and a woman in marriage to be foundational and for life (Matthew 19:1–9). The breaking of this relationship he viewed very seriously and in particular he highlighted the damage caused by adultery, even in one's thoughts (Matthew 5:27–32). Whilst Jesus does not go on to say that it is in the context of marriage that God intended children to be conceived, born and cared for, it is surely implied by the whole thrust of the Old Testament and by Jesus' endorsement of the marital relationship, plus his affirmation of children's responsibility to honour their parents.

Jesus constantly affirmed people in family. He spent time in different homes. He restored family relationships (eg Jairus' daughter, Lazarus, the Roman centurion's servant [not a relative please note] and the Canaanite woman's daughter). When small children were brought to him for his blessing, he returned them immediately into the care of those family members who had brought them, as this remained their responsibility. (Please note here the text does not say that parents were bringing their children but 'people' [Mark 10:13]. Given the nature of family life these could have been grandparents, aunts, uncles, older siblings or even neighbours, though no doubt some were parents.)

His teaching thus gives a key role to the marriage relationship within family life, but not an exclusive one. He endorses the role of parents in the care and nurture of their children (as he had himself experienced and submitted to), but others have roles to play. Then by upholding the fourth commandment, he shows that children have responsibilities to their families too. These are clearly not confined to childhood; the dispute recorded in Mark 7:9–13 is about this commandment being kept by adults with respect to their presumably ageing parents; the rich young ruler told Jesus that he had not given up keeping this commandment even though he was a young adult (Mark 10:19, 20). The clear implications are that for Jesus, family responsibilities had a lifelong nature for all parties concerned.

So, apparently by his own incarnation, life, actions and teaching, Jesus endorsed family life.

But this is not all. He also taught the provisional nature of marriage and family life when they are seen in the context of eternity. The marriage relationship is for this life; it does not extend into the next (Matthew 22:23–33). In no way does Jesus use this to devalue the role of marriage in this life. But what he says does act as a caution against arguing that marriage is an absolute state. This, I believe, can be linked to the Mosaic provision for divorce and Jesus' own apparent allowance for divorce in the case of adultery. If marriage was completely absolute there is no way any form of break-up or remarriage could ever be condoned. But within the context of a fallen world, with people who do fail, in the particular instance of actual (rather than mental) adultery, divorce (and, therefore, the concomitant possibility of remarriage) is allowable. The whole thrust of kingdom life and forgiveness would suggest that forgiveness and reconciliation should be the preferred and worked for route, but if this proves impossible, then divorce can follow. Grace, as God's good news, offering forgiveness, hope and fresh starts, must always triumph over law.

Jesus also makes it clear that family should not be the highest priority of all in life. He called people to leave everything in order that they might follow him and enter the kingdom. They were, above all else, to seek first God's kingdom and righteousness. This leaving everything included family, as he himself had had to do (Matthew 19:29). His disciples are seen to put this into practice. They did not abandon their families, as we can see from the regularity with which they were based back in Capernaum, but they did spend time away from them. When this was pointed out to Jesus he did not rebuke them for it but simply promised a reward (Mark 10:28–31). He was very straightforward in telling his disciples that the good news of the kingdom might actually lead to the break up of human families. There could be, in fact certainly would be, betrayal and hatred from family members for at least some of them (Mark 13:12; Luke 12:49–53).

Further, Jesus implied that in the kingdom there was in fact a more important family. Whilst his teaching suggested the provisional nature of family in this world, it also suggested the ongoing nature of God's family both in this world and on into eternity (Mark 10:29–30; 3:31–35).

None of this was to be used as an excuse for avoiding earthly responsibilities towards family members, particularly as laid down in the law (Mark 7:9–13). But it does need to be kept in mind, so that we see families and family life within the ultimate and greater context of God's kingdom and the family people to which he calls us all to belong through faith in Christ.

One further reflection on Christ's own ministry. He knew people who apparently lived in a wide range of family types: homes with only one child (Jairus); homes with none, indeed where perhaps no members were married (Mary, Martha and Lazarus); extended homes where servants lived (Roman centurion), or mothers-in-law (Peter), or grown up children (Zebedee); homes full of broken relationships (the woman of Samaria); homes where, possibly, someone lived alone (Zacchaeus). There is no endorsement or condemnation of any particular type or style of family. Jesus worked with families as they were, not as they might ideally have been. In this he was surely following the pattern that his Father had given him through the stories of God working in and through a whole host of families in the Old Testament. In this he acts as our model and guide.

Conclusions

The fact that God actually lived as a human being in a human family sets the seal on the value of the family and the importance of working with individuals within their family context. But it also warns us against being overly prescriptive about family types. It shows us the importance of recognising that family life is ever dynamic and that roles within the family change. Jesus' own place and role underwent a number of changes throughout his life, yet he always fulfilled them in complete perfection and never failed to meet his family responsibilities. But his teaching and example make abundantly clear the ultimate provisionality of the earthly family: in the light of God's rule and eternal family, it simply pales into the background.

If we are to reach families and family members for God, we will need to take them and their family very seriously, as Jesus did; but we will also need to introduce them to a greater and more wonderful family, the family of God. And they will only really begin to see this as members of that family seek to live out their real family life in their own families and communities – in other words, as they see God's people living as God's family day by day.

> **Stop**
>
> If you have not done so as you have read this chapter take time to look at the Bible references given.
>
> - Meditate either on Jesus' own family life or on his teaching.
> - What implications do you draw from your meditation?

5
GOD'S FAMILY PEOPLE

It is my firm conviction that at the heart of any outreach by a local church community or wider grouping of churches to families outside their community is their corporate life as God's family people.

Whilst all the chapters which follow this one will seek to offer ideas and models for ways of reaching families, if this 'heart' of the corporate life of God's family people is not right, I believe all the ideas and models will either completely fail or be far less effective than they ought to be. So let us take a look at how God has worked through his family people in biblical history and at the guidelines scripture offers us for how he might work through us today.

Through the Old Testament
In creation humankind as a whole was meant to express the family image of God and care for the created order. When that was fractured and distorted by Adam and Eve's decision to rebel against him, God did not give up on his original intention. In the execution of his plan to rescue the human family and creation from the ultimate consequences of human rebellion, he always chose to operate through a people, within which individuals played a highly important role. It seems that it was never a case of 'individuals' versus 'community', but always of each individual being highly significant within the broader context of

God's whole family people. Then this family itself fell within God's overall concern for the whole human family and created order. Let us unfold some of the history to illustrate this.

Noah

Noah and his family were to establish the re-made family of God after the flood, but by no means simply for their own benefit. The command, as it had been with Eve and Adam, was to fill the whole earth with Noah's own descendants. Within the context of the story, this meant all future human beings, because they would all be Noah's descendants. Hence the covenant with Noah and his descendants was and is with the whole human family. Noah, his wife, sons and daughters-in-law were individually significant because they believed God's word and responded in faith by building the ark and getting into it. They became significant as God's family people because of their obedience in re-populating the earth and being faithful to the God who not only made them but also rescued them. Yet God was not confined by a specific individual or family group; he worked corporately through this whole 'new' human family of God (Genesis 9:1–17).

Abraham

Abraham was clearly significant as an individual and his own faith actions mattered. But God's covenant promises to him and his family would bring about the blessing of all nations (Genesis 12:1–3). God's activity was not limited to a people related by kinship; his people were also to be related by promise and faith. By the time we reach the end of Abraham's life the family people of God were firmly established as those who shared in the faith commitment that they had to the Lord.

'Kinship family' (those related by blood and betrothal) was always intended to completely overlap with 'faith family' (those related by their common faith). But these relationships had been fractured with Cain and Abel and in every family thereafter. The stories of Noah, Abraham, Isaac and Jacob all illustrate that God worked his promises and purposes out through the 'faith family' from the rebellion of humankind onwards – a point very strongly picked up in the New Testament by Paul in Galatians and Romans, and by the writer of Hebrews. But before jumping ahead too quickly let us continue through the Old Testament.

Moses
The covenant made with Moses clearly affirmed the importance in God's purposes of the whole people of God as a family community through whom he acted to rescue the whole world. Israel was called 'a holy nation': God's own people called to live God's way in the midst of a world which chose to go its own way (Exodus 19:3–6). The whole Mosaic law was designed to help Israel live out its distinctive calling. Whilst there was a constant distancing from the surrounding nations in terms of lifestyle and worship, there was always openness and welcome to anyone and everyone who wanted to join them in their trust in God the Creator and Redeemer. Those who would join God's family by active faith needed no kinship relationship with the Hebrews; the faith family took priority over the kinship family. This is equally illustrated in the reverse. Where a kinship family member lost faith and actively rebelled against the Lord, then he or she had to be punished severely. The family of faith had to stay true to its holy calling, however costly that might have been in immediate kinship family terms. (This is perhaps best illustrated by the story of Moses, Aaron and Miriam in Numbers 12 and that of Achan in Joshua 6–7.)

The Prophets

The role of the prophets was that of calling God's people back to the task of being faithful to him; to shine as a light, showing the reality of God in the midst of the nations that surrounded them (Isaiah 42:6). Indeed at their most visionary, when they looked towards the day of the Lord, all the prophets held out a vision which was greater than Israel alone. They looked to the day when 'the earth will be full of the knowledge of the Lord as the waters cover the sea' (Isaiah 11:9; Habakkuk 2:14); when the whole created order would be renewed (Isaiah 65:17); when disgrace would be removed from all the earth (Isaiah 25:8); when such would be the presence of God in the midst of his worshipping people, that all the nations would be drawn to their maker (Micah 4).

Into the New Testament

Such, then, was the high calling laid on God's family people. Yet the calling was not lived out. Israel became concerned solely for its own welfare; the people became exclusive and lost sight of their global, even universal calling. But just as throughout the Old Testament God's ultimate purposes were never frustrated by human frailty, so in the New Testament God continues to use a people belonging to him and each other through faith, to act as the means by which he will reach the whole earth.

In the coming of Jesus the call of the people of God, Israel, was focussed in the one person. Israel was meant to be the light for the world, so the Son of God became that light (John 8:12). Israel was meant to be the servant of the Lord, so the Son became the servant (Matthew 12:17–21). The temple was meant to be the focus of worship so the Son's body became the temple (John 2:19–22). Indeed John graphically points out the nature of Jesus' ministry as the fulfilment of the calling of God's people (John 12:20–33). Up to this point in John's Gospel,

Jesus had been dealing directly with the Jews; but now, for the first time, gentiles sought him out. John depicts Jesus as recognising the significance of this in his role as the servant of the Lord: the gentiles were coming to him, just as they were meant to be drawn to God through his servant. This event, John implies, confirmed for Jesus that the time for the most important part of his ministry had arrived: now he had to die in order that all, not just those within Israel, might be drawn to him.

Jesus, however, did not leave it at this. He created around himself a family of faith, which had its most immediate expression amongst the twelve disciples and those who travelled with them. In this small community Jesus taught and demonstrated the values that belong to the people who live under the reign of God, who acknowledge him as their ruler, their Lord. Within this group there were those who were related by kinship (Peter and Andrew, James and John, and even possibly Jesus himself with these last two), but most were related by their faith commitment to Jesus as their teacher and Lord. We saw in the last chapter how Jesus' own teaching placed a higher priority on this faith relationship than he did on kinship. He was already doing what God's people were meant to do; he was drawing others to the Father and the community was expanding.

Within this context, he gave to his followers the clear instruction that they were now to take up the calling of Israel, to make the good news of God and his rule known throughout all the earth. They were now to be the light of the world and the salt of the earth (Matthew 5:13–16), the servants and messengers of the Lord and of his kingdom. After his death and resurrection he made it clearer than at any time during his public ministry that this calling was to all people in all nations. No longer was it to operate primarily within the confines of the nation of Israel, but actively to be taken to, proclaimed and lived out in all the nations of the earth (Matthew 28:18–20; Luke 24:47; Acts 1:8).

The disciples understood themselves and their mission in this way (though not without times of struggling to break free from their old nationalistic thinking). Peter, it appears, quickly accepted the inclusion of the Samaritans within the new family of faith, but took rather longer to accept the gentiles (Acts 8:14–25; 10:1–11:18). But by the time he came to write his first letter he describes the believing community, made up of gentiles and Jews, as the people of God, 'a holy nation' (1 Peter 2:9ff). Paul calls the followers of Jesus 'the Israel of God' and those who have been 'grafted' into God's people (Galatians 6:16; Romans 9–11). Those who place their faith in Christ are the true descendants and inheritors of Abraham, of the promises made to him and, therefore, of his calling (Romans 4; Galatians 3).

Thus it is that the earliest followers of Jesus saw themselves as God's family people called out by him to bear witness to his truth and grace. (The Greek word *ekklesia* means 'the called out ones', but it is usually translated 'church'.) Now it is through the church that the purposes of God are being revealed (Ephesians 3:10, 11). The church should live such an outgoing expression of the divine life that others are drawn and attracted to God in Christ through its witness. This is not to draw people to a church building; nor is it to make them into good church members; but it is to draw people to God in Christ for forgiveness, new life and adoption into the family of God.

Stop

Take time to read some of the texts given above and think about the calling of God's people to live out the corporate divine life here on earth.

The Life of God's Family People

The story of Acts is full of the proclaiming of the good news of God in Jesus. Yet surprisingly, perhaps, the epistles make far more of the ongoing life of God's people. There are very few calls to evangelise overtly, but there are numerous exhortations to live the life of God and to let that speak.

So Peter tells the scattered Christians to whom he writes that it is their good lives which will silence criticism and draw glory to God (1 Peter 2:11–12, 15,20; 3:1–17; 4:19; 2 Peter 1:3–9; 3:11–14). John reminds his readers that it is not what they say about love which counts, but actually living lives marked by loving actions (1 John 3:11–24, 4:19–21; 2 John 5–6). Paul, in his letters to the early Christians, constantly teaches that their lives must be worthy of the God who has called them (Ephesians 4:1; Philippians 1:27; 1 Thessalonians 2:12). It is the consistency of their lives and their life together which will win the respect of others (Colossians 4:5–6; 1 Thessalonians 4:11–12).

A telling phrase, showing the importance of this community life, is 'one another' (1 John 3:11). Just as in the Godhead there is constant movement towards one another, so too should there be in the life of God's people. In the home life of Christians living together, and in the community life of believers from a number of households, the love of God expressed in love for one another should become plain. The powerful dynamic of this life towards one another is illustrated simply by listing those things which are included in it:

> LOVE one another (John 13:34–35; Roman 12:10; 1 Thessalonians 4:9; 1 Peter 1:22; 1 John 3:11; 4:7, 11, 21)
> HONOUR one another (Romans 12:10)
> LIVE IN HARMONY WITH one another (Romans

12:16; 15:5)
ACCEPT one another (Romans 15:7)
BUILD UP one another (1 Thessalonians 5:11)
GREET one another (Romans 16:16; 2 Corinthians 13:12)
SERVE one another (Galatians 5:13)
CARRY one another's BURDENS (Galatians 6:2)
BE KIND TO one another (Ephesians 4:32)
BE PATIENT WITH one another (Ephesians 4:2)
SUBMIT TO one another (Ephesians 5:21)
FORGIVE one another (Colossians 3:13)
CONFESS YOUR SINS TO one another (James 5:16)
ENCOURAGE one another (Hebrews 3:13)

All of these flow out from the first ('Love one another ...'), and arise because of the total conviction that in Christ all believers are intimately joined together as members of Christ's one body (1 Corinthians 12). There are also things which Christians are called not to do to one another like provoking, envying and judging (Galatians 5:26; Romans 14:13). The community life of God's people should be apparent in the relationships between husbands and wives, parents and children; in the life of work; in family and household contexts; as well as between believers from different households, regardless of their economic or social background.

This may sound rather idyllic, but is it really? The corporate life of the early church clearly struck the community around it and attracted many to find out more (Acts 2:42–47; 4:32–37; 1 Thessalonians 1:7–10). This was not without its problems, but these were confronted and successful solutions found (Acts 6:1–7). In addition, their life together cannot be regarded as idyllic because it includes within it the reality of failure and human frailty. Where else would you need confession, forgiveness, patience, encouragement, respect, building up and kindness if it is

God's family people

not in a community that sometimes fell into mutual judging, envy, gossip . . .

The mark of the Christian family and of Christians within families is that, whilst they can fail just the same as everyone else, they are different because they have discovered the God who loves and forgives and they have begun to show love and forgiveness towards one another as well. It is this difference that knowing Jesus Christ makes which ought to mark out the local church from the rest of the community. As others see it, experience it and consider it in the lives of Christian neighbours, workmates and households so they will want to know more about the God who is behind it all. As Christians serve their local communities in seeking the welfare of the families and households in their neighbourhoods, so they will automatically be evangelistic and will reach families for Christ. People are crying out for such community. The people of God are in a position to demonstrate it because they know the God of community and have the Spirit of God within them to bring it about in their daily lives.

Putting it into Practice

There can be no set pattern or formula for putting this life style into practice. It will vary from culture to culture, district to district, and will even take on different forms within one local church setting. This is part of its beauty. It is absolutely adaptable to the needs of each local community and therefore adaptable for reaching different family types. What we all have to do is constantly seek ways of putting the principle into effect.

Sara came from a background in another faith. She had married young and had children early. Life in her home was far from happy. Her husband never treated her with any respect and on occasions became physically violent towards her. She, however, remained faithful and sought to be a 'good' wife and mother. When the third child came along, however, the husband owned up to having had an affair with another woman, and left Sara with the three small children. He still regularly reappeared 'to have his conjugal rights' but otherwise became an absentee father. Understandably the depression that Sara had developed deepened further and she lived in constant fear of her husband's violence and of social 'disgrace'.

One day a Christian aquaintance (no more than that), finding her in such a state, expressed genuine concern. Suddenly the whole story spilt out. Initially the Christian was shocked, lost for words or action. But she invited Sara to join her at a church prayer meeting where she was sure the minister would pray for Sara and her situation. Sara, surprising herself, went along. She felt completely at sea in this totally alien environment and yet she also sensed the reality of God and a warmth of welcome from the prayer group that she had never experienced before.

Now this group of Christians would readily acknowledge that they were full of weaknesses and made mistakes, yet God used them to express his love and concern to Sara. Over the weeks, indeed months that followed, they visited Sara, helped her with shopping, cleaning, child care, legal advice, finance, and generally loved her. She was much prayed for and with. After some months the warmth of God's people led Sara to commit her own life to Jesus as Saviour and Lord. She follows him to this day though the journey has been filled with some nightmarish experiences which have led to periods of doubt, even outright disbelief. Through them all, the care of God's family people has held fast and enabled her and her children to grow in Christian faith.

Sara's story shows that God's love can be shared through his people in a whole host of ways. There is one aspect, however, that I want to highlight particularly – that of hospitality. Paul told the Romans to 'practise hospitality' (Romans 12:13). Peter said that Christians were to offer hospitality to one another without grumbling (1 Peter 4:9). John commended the hospitality of Gaius (3 John 5–8). The writer to the Hebrews commended being hospitable to strangers (Hebrews 13:2). And Paul said that a mark of a church leader should be their hospitality (1 Timothy 3:2).

Hospitality is linked linguistically in the New Testament with two ideas: the first is of loving friendship; the second is of entertaining strangers (in the sense of welcoming them into the home and giving them a meal). Surely both these aspects of hospitality are crucial in reaching families outside of the church. Are the homes of church members places where next door neighbours can be sure of a friendly reception? Are they places where strangers will be invited in and made to feel at home? They certainly ought to be. The home of a single person can be a place of warmth and friendship to a family of four, just as much as the other way around. A Christian household should be a place where an individual or family group from a different ethnic background sense a love and concern that contrasts with the racism they might perceive elsewhere. We need to ask ourselves some searching questions. How often do we invite others into our homes for a meal or just a coffee? Do our children play with others in the neighbourhood and make new friendships? Do we help out with shopping, household chores or lifts? Do we seek to offer help whenever we are aware someone has been ill or had a new baby? Do we offer comfort at times of bereavement? Do we help celebrate in times of joy? Are we basically people with open hearts and open homes?

Iris lost her husband through lung cancer. The local curate visited her before the funeral and again afterwards. Several things about her circumstances struck the curate as similar to those of Doris, a regular member of the church with a delightful faith marked by gentleness and kindness. The curate asked Doris to call on Iris just 'to say hello'. From this simple beginning, the two became good friends and started doing things together. They offered each other real companionship. Eventually Iris decided to join Doris at church one Sunday morning; she had hardly been since childhood. What struck her was the welcome that some children gave her. Her own grandchildren lived many miles away and she was only able to see them very occasionally. These children gradually became her surrogate grandchildren.

Then Iris herself developed terminal cancer; it was a long and painful way to die. But Doris was still there, and the children, and her own 'kinship family', and the curate. Through all the months that followed, Iris found herself first beginning to pray, then becoming convinced that God was listening and was with her. In her dying days she found a deep peace in knowing that Jesus was with her and was waiting for her 'on the other side'. 'I know he is there and that he died for me, I can die in peace,' she said. And shortly after, she did. What had led her to such faith was the open hearts of those whom she had met.

What about hospitality in church? When a stranger does pluck up the courage to come to a church event, whether it be a regular worship service or a social evening, do we make them feel welcome? Or do church members sit in their cliques and only talk with each other?

Or when church members are involved in local community groups and activities (as they should be), are they the people who take the lead in offering friendship and welcome? Do they stand out as the ones with something positively different about them? This does not mean everyone turning into extroverts; some will be like that by virtue of their personalities, others will not. It is about attitude and action; an introvert can be just as loving and welcoming as an extrovert. They simply have different ways of showing it.

> **Stop**
>
> Consider the place of hospitality in your own life and the life of your church.
> - What is good about it already?
> - What could be improved and how?

The life of a church community is meant to be primarily about *relationship*: relationship first with the Lord, but also relationship with each other. Yet how many church services and meetings actually function with these as key factors? Most churches seem to be overly business-like and not enough 'fellowship-like'. They run more like organisations than living organisms, and more like social clubs than alternative societies. The church is meant to exist to communicate and share the love and life of Almighty God with the world. Yet so many churches are so busy with their internal affairs that members never have time to make friendships with their neighbours, get involved with their local community or even develop healthy hobbies. We need to ensure that we so structure local fellowships that there is time and energy to make friendships with families and individuals outside the church. This may mean a revolution in how some churches are structured; if so it will be a revolution long overdue.

Reaching families

> **Stop**
>
> Consider the life of your local church.
>
> - In what ways is it based on relationship? With God? With each other? With the local community? With the needs of the wider world?
>
> - Are there ways of creating change to improve all these relationships?

6

FAMILY LIFE OPPORTUNITIES

The birth of a child, the death of a parent, marriage, moving house, being made redundant, divorce and serious illness are all key points in the lives of individuals and family groupings. They can be times of joy and wonder, anxiety, doubt, fear or despair. It is quite common that at such times individuals and families together find themselves asking questions about life, its purpose and meaning; questions which at other times have never really passed through their minds or which have been pushed to one side as not important, or as too much to deal with whilst life is jogging along quite happily.

Naturally these events affect the whole family or household unit, and the extended family connections. Then each individual will react to the event in a different way because of their age, experience, specific involvement and so forth. We need to see these moments as opportunities for bringing the wholeness of God's love into people's lives where previously it has been ignored or rejected. As God's people we should be sharing in the joy and wonder, caring in the times of sorrow and bringing hope where it seems to have gone. We should do this purely out of love for each family and person, wanting the best for them. If people choose to want to have nothing to do with Jesus, we should not stop caring and loving.

These kinds of events are part of what is described as the Family Life Cycle. This is common to a greater or lesser degree to all families and it's helpful to be aware of it. Sometimes events and feelings arise which overly spiritual pundits put down to all sorts of spiritual reasons, when in fact they are simply part of everyone's life cycle pattern. This cycle helps us understand the phases which families go through, and to identify the particular needs of individuals within the family because of where they are in the cycle. This in turn can help us understand some of the inevitable tensions which arise within every family. There are likely to be three generational groups somewhere in the family make-up, at three different developmental stages with different emotional and psychological needs. These bring great enough tensions without the additional and disturbing trauma of something like bereavement through death or divorce.

Inevitably, every specific family's cycle has something unique about it. For example, having a child in adolescence throws the spiral, as illustrated, out of tilt: it brings together adolescence and childbirth, possibly having skipped over marriage/courtship. If this new-born child were to follow the same pattern, the mother actually reaches grandparenthood before reaching the 're-evaluation of life' stage, which occurs for many people in their forties when the children are going through adolescence and about to leave home.

This life cycle pattern applies to Christians just as much as non-Christians. The processes, emotions, changes and stages are no different. Once again it offers an opportunity for Christians in families to demonstrate to others that they are just the same, yet different because of the presence of the Father, the Son and the Spirit in their lives.

It is actually quite staggering how many people include in their own personal story of coming to faith in Christ the place that a significant life event had in the process. Let us take a closer look at how the church might find

Family life opportunities

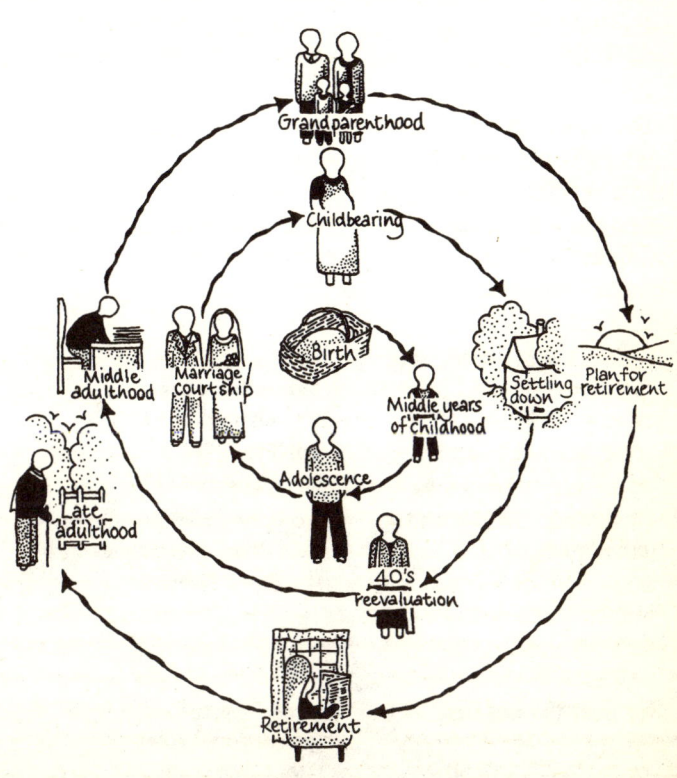

Fig 2 The Family Life Spiral

Fig 3 The Stages of the Family Life Cycle

Family Life Cycle Stage	Emotional Process of Transition: Key Principles
1. Leaving home: Single young adults	Accepting emotional and financial responsibility for self
2. The joining of families through marriage: The new couple	Commitment to new system
3. Families with young children	Accepting new members into the system
4. Families with adolescents	Increasing flexibility of family boundaries to include children's independence and grandparents' frailties
5. Launching children and moving on	Accepting a multitude of exits from and entries into the family system
6. Families in later life	Accepting the shifting of generational roles

Second-Order Changes in Family Status
Required to Proceed Developmentally

a. Differentiation of self in relation to family of origin
b. Development of intimate peer relationships
c. Establishment of self rework and financial independence.

a. Formation of marital system
b. Realignment of relationships with extended families and friends to include spouse

a. Adjusting marital system to make space for child(ren)
b. Joining in childrearing, financial, and household tasks
c. Realignment of relationships with extended family to include parenting and grandparenting roles

a. Shifting of parent–child relationships to permit adolescents to move in and out of the system
b. Refocus on mid-life marital and career issues
c. Beginning shift toward joint caring for older generation

a. Renegotiation of marital system as a dyad
b. Development of adult-to-adult relationships between grown children and their parents
c. Realignment of relationships to include in-laws and grandchildren
d. Dealing with disabilities and death of parents (grandparents)

a. Maintaining own and/or couple functioning and interests in face of physiological decline; exploration of new familial and social role options
b. Support for a more central role of middle generation.
c. Making room in the system for the wisdom and experience of the elderly, supporting the older generation without overfunctioning for them
d. Dealing with loss of spouse, siblings, and other peers and preparation for own death; life review and integration

itself presented with God-given opportunities to share Christ with families through 'natural' events.

Birth

Having a baby is a wonderful event. Certainly there is plenty of unpleasantness and pain for many women through pregnancy and childbirth, but for most people there is wonder and joy at a new-born child. You only have to look at proud new parents or the way a group reacts to a new baby to see this. This sense of wonder and joy affects all family members: parents, grandparents, siblings and so on.

It is often also a time of anxiety. 'How will I/we cope as parents?' 'Will the grandparents interfere?' 'How will my son/daughter cope with their new brother/sister?' 'Should I help or will I be seen as interfering?' 'Will Mummy love me as much now that there is a new baby in the home?' These are just some of the anxieties that arise for different 'family' members.

Here Christian neighbours and friends should be able to offer friendship and support. If opportunities arise to talk about the wonder or the anxieties, then Christians should naturally share their thoughts and feelings about God's involvement and concern with all of this. They can offer to pray in thanksgiving or for people's fears. They can simply, naturally and in an unforced way share Christ.

When Mark's wife had their first baby and it developed breathing problems he was amazed by Peter's understanding and willingness to listen. Peter, heart-in-mouth, offered to pray for Mark, his wife and baby, half-expecting a sharp response or smack in the mouth; he actually received a slightly startled but welcoming 'yes'. It was a brief prayer and Mark was rather embarrassed by it, but meant it when he said, 'Thanks, I kind of feel less worried already.' A friendship deepened that day. Mark, so far as I know, is

Family life opportunities

still not committed to Christ, but he has a healthier view of Christians, prayer and God. His journey to faith continues.

Some parents will want to go further with their new baby. Something inside of them will want to express thanks to something or someone greater than themselves; they may well think of God. They may also want to give the new life over to this someone. So they may approach the church 'officially' for a baptism or thanksgiving or dedication.

It is very easy for ministers and other church leaders to act negatively at this point feeling that this is more 'folk religion' than Christian faith. It often is. However, it may also be evidence of the Spirit of God at work in this person or family's life. A wholly negative reaction could well convince the enquirers never to come near this church, or any other for that matter, ever again. A positive response might be the next step towards seeing a family, or at least some within it, finding faith in Christ for themselves.

This does not mean a wide open infant baptism policy in churches which practice this or a wide open dedication policy in churches which practice adult baptism. It does mean, however, an openness to providing some form of thanksgiving for the safe delivery of the child and prayer for her and her family. There is an opportunity to spend time with the family in their own home, talking over what it is exactly they are looking for, explaining the reasons for Christian dedication or baptism and the spiritual responsibilities of parents and other family members, alongside the responsibilities and help which the local church is willing to offer. This may well include inviting the new parents to join a parenting group, or trying out an outsider-friendly (and baby-friendly!) all-age service. It will mean having a church which is welcoming and hospitable towards new families as they come into contact with the fellowship. It will also mean patience.

Roy and Trisha had their first child early on in their marriage. They had married in church but otherwise had never been since childhood. Yet with a new baby they wanted to do something to say thank you to the God who they believed was probably there. The thought of a child growing and developing from a sperm and an egg, and the awe of the birth made them convinced it was near miraculous. So they approached a church to have their child 'done'.

They were welcomed by the minister who visited their home a couple of times to explain about the Christian faith and baptism. They were pleasantly surprised that she was 'normal' and they were genuinely fascinated by the Christian story. They even went to church to the regular all-age service. The crèche helped; so did the relaxed atmosphere, the announcement of page numbers in the books and the tea and coffee afterwards. (They did not stay as they felt very self-conscious, but the fact that it happened impressed them.) The baptism was a happy event. There were only two babies being 'done' that day and the minister made the occasion feel special for them. But they did not go again.

Eighteen months later a second child arrived. Quite quickly they decided to get in touch with the vicar again. She remembered them; they were amazed. This time they went a little more often and even stayed for coffee on some occasions. One or two other church members also apparently remembered them and talked with them, not about church, to their relief, but about babies and homes and work. The second baptism felt a little more special; somehow both Roy and Trisha felt it meant a little more this time around. Trisha started going along to a parent and toddler group run at the church. She and the children enjoyed the occasional pram services as well. But Sunday worship dropped off after the baptism.

With the third child, however, something began to 'click' as they both put it. Sundays at church became a regular feature and when a chance to join a small group exploring the Christian faith arose they both joined it. Confirmation followed, when they expressed their genuine longing to follow Christ. Today the whole family is seeking to welcome others in the way that they were warmly, but unthreateningly, welcomed on the birth of their first child.

Many families have come to Christ because of a first contact like this one. Inevitably some parents and children will never be seen again, yet even for these we have been fulfilling part of our calling by welcoming them. Openness, welcome and friendship will affirm people as human beings; it will aid the bringing of God's wholeness into their lives and in some way convey God's grace to each family member, whether or not they respond to it.

Marriage
Large numbers of people still approach churches (particularly the Church of England) for weddings. Too many ministers just book the wedding in, run a brief rehearsal, take the ceremony and leave it at that. Marriage is a huge commitment. Everyone approaching it has questions, uncertainties, fears and hopes. Yet where do they have a chance to express these or find help with them? Here, at the outset of the establishment of a new 'family unit' is an opportunity for showing God's love. If nothing else, helping a couple prepare for this new step will give them a far better chance of staying together and developing a good family life within their own home. It may also lead to Christian faith and commitment.

Good marriage preparation should, therefore, be a standard part of every church's practice. It will help to establish godly standards in marriage relationships and may help some find Christ. Such marriage preparation needs to give time to the particular questions and anxieties of each couple, rather than simply follow some set formula laid down by church leaders. It also needs to be honest and realistic. There is no point in running such preparation on the assumption that everyone is a virgin before marriage. It is highly likely that most couples coming for marriage preparation will have had sexual intercourse with previous partners, friends or acquaintances and that they are already having sexual intercourse together (including at least some, if not many, Christian couples). Large numbers will be cohabiting and may have been doing so for quite a while. To come down heavily on such people at the outset, by saying that what they are doing is sinful and they need to begin with repentance, is hardly the best way to approach them. There may indeed need to be confession, repentance, forgiveness and renewal as part of their journey together, but it is not usually the best place to start.

The same applies where one or other of the partners is already divorced. Pastoral sensitivity and thought needs to enter our approach. It should not and cannot be ignored, but nor should it become an automatic block to help and support. Many ministers may well feel unable to actually re-marry divorcees in many or all contexts, but that should not exclude the possibility of advising, helping and praying for this new partnership.

Ann had not been married before, but Winston had. Understandably Ann felt that to be denied a wedding in church because of her partner's previous wife's unfaithfulness was unfair on her, if not Winston as well. After careful conversations, Ann understood the position of the minister who did not wish to conduct the marriage service in church but was willing to offer a service of prayer and blessing after a civil marriage. He was also willing to help the couple think through marriage – its meaning and purpose – and to help them face some of the issues that would confront them. Whilst not totally convinced, the warmth of concern and genuine willingness to help led Ann and Winston to agree to this format.

They were surprised by the openness of the couple who took their marriage preparation sessions (not the minister and his wife but a trained couple from the congregation). It was refreshing to find such honesty, and yet here were a couple still happily married and clearly in love. It was also gratifying not to have the Bible thrust down their throats; it was used and referred to, but in a straightforward and helpful way. In fact they were surprised at some of the material in the Bible (the Song of Solomon completely bowled them over). The service of blessing went well (in Ann and Winston's, and their relatives' and friends' eyes). But they were not seen in church again, until two years later when their first child was expected.

Then continued a story of baptism enquiry and preparation. Over the next few years Ann came to a living faith which has flourished ever since. Ten years on, Winston is just becoming warm to such a faith himself in a different place with a different group of God's people, a group who have been as welcoming as the first. Whether or not he ever comes to faith, one thing is clear. The marriage and home life show all the marks of relationships run along Christian lines; it is a household of honesty, forgiveness, fun, love, patience and kindness from which the children and many others have benefited. The care in preparation has brought many benefits.

Where one or both partners have been previously married, children from the first partnership may be involved. Much time and thought should be given to them. How do they feel? What support and help might we offer as they wrestle with changes and tensions because of the proposed re-marriage of their parent? In the creation of a blended family there is more preparatory work to be done and the people of the gospel ought to be involved.

Marriage is used widely in the Bible as a symbol of the relationship between God and his people, of Christ and the church. This very fact should alert us to the potential of marriage for sharing the good news with families. Failure to take this opportunity is to everyone's loss.

Some kind of after-service care should be included as well. Many find a six month check-up invaluable, just to iron out any difficulties that may be arising. (Many enter marriage saying they will have none, but have changed their tune in six months!) This kind of care might be what takes this family one step further on towards discovering God.

Divorce

When divorce happens it causes great traumas to all family members. Logically Christians should be working for the upholding of the marriage relationship and encouraging those who face difficulties in their marriage partnership (and every couple has them at some time) to work through the differences and difficulties together. Confession, repentance, forgiveness and no holding of grudges should be regular parts of every family's life. Church leaders should be considering what support can be given to marriages to help them grow, develop, mature and stay together rather than break up. Are church members so busy with church meetings that they do not have adequate times for being with their partners? Is there a great enough openness about communication in marriage? Or about the ups and downs of sexual intercourse? In a culture which portrays sex as always pleasurable, always ecstatic and taking place highly frequently, does not the church have a role to play in being honest about some of the difficulties that virtually all couples actually experience in the sexual side of their relationship? But how often do we actually teach or discuss this?

Shouldn't churches tackle much more openly the issues

of how sexuality develops in children and through adolescence? And instead of simply saying to single people (all of whom have sexual feelings and urges) 'no sexual intercourse', shouldn't they rather help them to explore how their sexuality can be expressed appropriately? So churches need to work harder at helping people to enjoy their singleness or to enjoy their marriage for life. They need to be more positive in encouraging marriages to develop rather than shouting, 'No divorce.'

Yet even so, some marriages do go wrong. Divorce does happen, and in the midst of it people are hurt. Surely the followers of Christ ought to love and help families through such traumas with practical support through child care, counselling, legal advice, a bed for the night or even a box of tissues. Judgement and condemnation have little place or meaning when someone is in the throes of a marriage break-up. Compassion and support fit better with a gospel of grace at such times.

Death

The death of a family member is an event which cries out for pastoral care and support. The grief and grieving process are important in helping those who have suffered the loss come to terms with life without their partner, parent, child, friend. Bereavement affects every single family member. Christians should be there as shoulders to cry on, listening ears, makers of tea, shoppers and gentle pray-ers.

Bereavement is not a time to come in with heavy evangelistic thrusts. However, it is a time when people ask questions about life and death. Once again these act as a window into a new way of looking at the world; an opportunity for the gospel to shine through. Yet seeing a funeral as 'just another task to be done' is sadly all too common amongst ministers. It may be a minister's tenth funeral that week, but for the family this is their only loss and it is felt deeply; the minister must treat each funeral and each family with love, time and care.

As people come through the initial shock and anger, so their questions will form more fully. It is therefore in the ongoing bereavement care and counselling that real opportunities to share Christ are most likely. It is just at this point where so many churches fail. Ministers and church members may well be very good around the time of death and immediately after the funeral, but what about a few weeks later when the pain and grief remain but there is no one now showing concern? We must look at befriending and helping those who have been bereaved on a much longer term basis than has normally been done. Christians should be going the extra several miles.

Julie, a single parent, lost her third child at only two weeks old. The whole community around her offered sympathy, did shopping, collected and cared for the older children for the first month after it happened. Then one by one they all dropped away. Two Christians, who had not been close friends before, did not give up. They continued to visit regularly, took the children out, baby-sat so that Mum could go out with her boyfriend occasionally, and cried with Julie. Julie even went to church a few times but could never cope with sitting still for so long. As time went by, these Christians became really good friends with Julie. One of them was single, the other married with his own children. Julie relied on them, but also helped them in different ways too. It was not all one way. They often talked about God and Julie clearly changed her views on God's reality, Jesus' life, death and resurrection. Her faith seemed to develop, but she never could cope with church, nor could her older children.

It is important to remember that every family member is affected in a bereavement, not just the most immediate relatives. We need wherever possible to offer help and counsel to as wide a range of the family as we are able.

God's Spirit may be at work in those in whom we least expect it. Such care around death must be offered in and for its own sake. But we need to be aware of the openings for the good news which may arise, and make the most of these.

Redundancy and Unemployment

At whatever age it happens redundancy is a highly traumatic event. When someone is young, it can give them a sense of failure and hopelessness. It will often place a family under great stress because of the financial worries that ensue and the tensions that it can create between family members. When it happens later in life, it is arguably even more disturbing to both the individual and the family. Someone who has given many years service to their skill or profession, perhaps to one particular firm or company, can be devastated. The trauma in all cases can lead to asking deep questions: 'Am I over the hill or on the scrap heap at forty nine?' 'All these years of graft, and what for? It all seems a waste.' 'Will I ever work again?'

So often the very purpose and meaning of a person's life has been tied up with their work. Now these things have been taken away. The trauma may be even greater if redundancy is tied to other life-changing events as well. A young person may be thinking about a life partnership, or have recently begun one; or have recently had a child whom they naturally wish to provide for. A person in their forties may be facing the prospect of their children leaving home, and questions about the ongoing nature of their marriage may be arising. Someone in their fifties may be becoming a grandparent for the first time.

Christians may be facing these problems themselves. Surely good pastoral support from neighbours and friends is essential. There may even be a place for churches to be involved in job clubs, retraining, or employment advice. There have been successful support groups established by some churches for families coping with these issues. This support should be given for its own sake, yet, as the deeper questions of life are asked, people may discover that these are times when there is a fresh openness to the good news.

Retirement

When a couple have learnt to live with one or both going out to work every day, suddenly to have one or both at home all the time can bring new stresses and strains into their relationship. The wider family notices it too: grandparents now have extra time and would like to help with their grandchildren more, but such attention may be unwanted or resented by the parents.

The arrival of retirement can also highlight the nearness of death and lead to questions about the value of all that has gone before. The church community again needs to be there caring, loving and demonstrating the heart of life and the hope of the resurrection.

A Pastorally Evangelistic Community

All that has been written in this chapter may often be thought of as pastoral care rather than evangelism. My contention is that the divide between these two facets of Christian ministry is often put across in too stark a fashion. Pastoral care shown to those outside of the church family reveals the truth that God is concerned for and involved in the harsh realities of life and its ups and downs. Active pastoral care at such times is probably the key evangelistic tool that a church has. It will need a church that is in touch with its local community and which has people committed to serving families and individuals within that community. Visiting should be high on the agenda. As one clergyman has said when asked the secret of his church's growth: 'First, visiting; second, visiting; and third, visiting.'

This pastoral evangelism will involve groups designed to meet specific needs and an awareness that all these life issues affect every member of a family in some way or another. To help one family member is to help them all to some degree; but to help them together as a family will be even better.

People who are visited and cared for may well need further help to come to mature faith. This may be through personal witness, the loan of a book or video, or by taking part in a group exploring the Christian faith such as a Christian Basics or Alpha course. But this will only be the final part of a much longer story of pastoral care which communicates the good news by demonstrating God's love in action.

Stop

Take time to look back over some of the 'life opportunities' highlighted in this chapter.

- What use are you/is your church making of these opportunities currently?
- What could you/your church do to improve this?
- What do you think about the idea of pastoral evangelism?

Further Reading

Restructuring Family Values, Anne Borrowdale, SPCK, 1994. (Contains helpful sections on cohabiting, divorce.)

7
PARENTING

Parenthood is wonderfully exciting. It is also an enormous privilege when one remembers that one in eight couples are unable to have children. The emotions connected with excitement and privilege are very quickly joined by the feelings of responsibility that come with being a parent. Before long every parent finds themselves feeling inadequate. At least, if you have met someone for whom this is not true, I would like you to introduce them to me. The reason is straightforward. The whole event is brand new; there is no precedent. Even where a parent has helped look after a sibling, neighbour's child or simply baby-sat, the experience of caring for one's own child is quite different. It is scary. The baby seems so fragile and so utterly dependent. I have seen apparently irresponsible teenagers transformed into highly caring, responsible people almost literally overnight when they have become parents. But they have worried and fretted, been filled with all kinds of questions and doubts about their abilities – just like their older counterparts.

In past generations the new parent was less isolated from support than they tend to be today. Grandparents, brothers and sisters with children and other family members would often be living under the same roof or at least just along the lane in the village. Also, new parents had usually known children, handled babies, changed nappies and seen children at every stage of development.

Today in Western urbanised societies the situation is very different. Parents are often a long way from the grandparents or any other blood family members. They are therefore often away from the natural educators when it comes to parenting. Historically grandparents offered advice and support to new parents; they helped with feeding, sleeping, clothing, changing nappies and all the other basic matters which seem to dominate the first phase of parenting. Many new parents today have grown up in a situation where for many years they have been isolated from anything other than cursory contact with babies or younger children. The help offered through ante-natal classes, and by midwives and health visitors after the birth is vital. Yet this kind of help is not the same as having someone almost on call twenty-four hours a day or the experience of one's own lifetime contact with babies and children.

So here is an area of need and support for families that churches ought to be addressing. What could they be doing?

Parentcraft Training

The parentcraft classes run by local health authorities are excellent. Churches should encourage anyone with whom they have contact to make the most of these opportunities to learn. There may even be occasions when the church can offer its premises for the running of such classes.

However, for most parents the real problems start arising after the birth of the child. The lessons learnt before birth will be invaluable in the initial stages of adjusting to being a parent. But what about the times it does not work out as expected? What about all the questions that arise with the growing baby and child when there are no health care workers readily available? And where do you go for training in parentcraft when it is no longer a baby or a toddler that you are parenting but an awkward teenager or squabbling siblings?

Churches have a wealth of experience to offer in the form of parents, grandparents, maybe health care professionals, nursery nurses, teachers or social workers. They could certainly put together a series of parentcraft training sessions which would be of equal value to parents within and outside the life of the church community. In this way believers and non-believers will be meeting together as complete equals; just being a Christian does not make you a better parent! People will naturally share and learn together, friendships will develop and possibly non-church parents will begin to ask questions about Jesus and about being part of God's family for themselves.

There are a growing number of resources available to help in running series like these and they are listed at the close of the chapter. But resources are just that; they are not cure-alls or substitutes for your own planning and expertise.

Stop

Think about the needs of parents in your own church and neighbourhood.

- What help in Parentcraft training might your church be able to provide?

Some guidelines
The following guidelines should help in the thinking through of any parentcraft training regardless of which resources are used.

Reaching families

Determining the needs

1 Even if you are a parent yourself do not assume that you can determine the needs of the parents in your church or area. Before finalising any programme, ask a number of parents to express their own needs and involve them in every aspect of planning a programme. This will help you decide whether or not to run a group for parents with children of all ages or whether to focus on a particular age range (eg teenagers). It will also help you decide on the content of the course and what resources you will need to use, what 'experts' you may wish to invite to assist you and what style of course would be most appropriate.

2 Experience shows that the following subjects come up regularly, but please do not simply use this list without checking it out; some feature more regularly than others and each has their own nuances depending on the local area.

Discipline. The problem with discipline is that it tends to be very negative. The heart of this concern is the 'What?' the 'How?' and the 'Why?' of setting boundaries for children at different stages of their development. All children need and want clear boundaries, but parents need to learn how to determine them and then how to maintain them. Into this context come questions of reward and punishment. The aim of discipline is surely to help each child develop self-control in the context of respect for others; it is not about parents 'controlling' their children as if they owned them.

Development. Parents tend to worry a great deal about whether or not their child is developing as they should. Are they sitting, walking, talking, reading, making friends, beginning menstruation, masturbating, starting to shave, and so on, as and when 'they should'? This anxiety often stems from a basic lack of knowledge about the nature of child development at all its levels (physical, mental, emotional, moral, social and spiritual). It is remarkable how persistent old wives' tales and other myths can be in a so-called developed society.

In particular, the spiritual dimension of a child's life and spiritual development are widely unrecognised and ignored in secular training, although this is now beginning to change. Non-believing parents struggle especially, therefore, with their growing child's ability to wonder, their God-talk and musings about life, death and purpose. To include discussion on this area of development is thus pertinent to believing and non-believing parents and will sometimes stir their own spirituality afresh as well.

Play. Parents realise that play is very important for children. But 'Why?' and 'How?' are often questions they ask. The crucial connection between play and learning is not always understood. And because parents have often lost the art of playing themselves, they do not know how to play with their children. Society tends to portray play as childish rather than childlike. Play is in fact essential for the health of people of all ages. Take a look at the refreshment and renewal which occurs in people through taking part in sport, or relaxing over a good book. Think about the therapeutic value of watching a play or a film or going for a stroll in the countryside. Play is great: we all do it to some extent and we all need to do it for our own health and development. So do children.

It is into this area of play that television, video, video games, computers and computer games might be placed. They can all be positively valuable as means of play, though the content of some is harmful. Making judgments about their use therefore needs to be based on the content rather than the medium itself.

School and Schooling. Most parents are deeply concerned about their child's education. What makes a good school?

Reaching families

What can I expect of the school? What can I do at home to help with my child's education? What about allowing my child to take part in festivals from the Hindu, Sikh and Muslim faiths? What about RE and Sex Education? What about a job/career for my child? Help and advice in all these areas is generally warmly welcomed by parents from a wide range of backgrounds.

These four subjects arise again and again when parents are asked about their key concerns. A further one which has increasingly emerged in recent years is that of **sexuality**. What can I do to ensure that my child grows up with a healthy view of themselves? How can I make sure that my child does not grow up to be 'gay'? (This clearly reveals the persistent homophobia in our society.) Whilst sexuality is not so universally raised by parents, it probably would be number five on the current list.

A further concern where parents have more than one child is that of sibling differences and rivalry. This becomes an even more significant issue in a blended family.

It will be obvious that all these subjects could be covered in one session each or in a series of sessions, depending on the depth to which they are going to be taken. In an introductory course one week per subject is almost certainly wise, but if the group decides to go on for longer, particular issues may need to be covered in greater detail.

Planning Carefully

1 Do not choose the time which is best for you. Ask potential participants when is the best time for them. If there are parents with young children they may prefer early evening rather than later, or maybe Sunday afternoon.

2 Decide also what child-care will be offered. If there are two parents, aim to have both of them at the group. If this is to happen, they will need someone to look after their child(ren), as will the single parent. So are there people available who will baby/child-sit (eg older people, single people or couples without children)? Or will you arrange to have child-care facilities at a central point for all the children of the group?

3 How long will the course last for? People are far more likely to join a short life group than an open-ended one. Six weekly sessions is probably adequate in the first instance. If people want to go on, then re-plan accordingly when that request arises.

4 If you plan to use a published resource check it out carefully beforehand and make sure you have everything you need at each session (eg video, TV, pens, paper). If you want to invite someone in to help facilitate the group on a particular subject, invite them in good time and brief them fully.

5 Make sure that you have someone who can lead the group well, taking note of the varied backgrounds of the participants. These are not sessions to be turned into evangelistic addresses; they are to be about parenting.

6 Produce personal invitations for parents. They are far more likely to come if specifically and personally invited rather than through a general invitation in the church notices or church magazine. (How many non-church folk do these two avenues actually reach anyway?)

Running the Course

1 The key element in running the course is to recognise the value and skills which already exist within the group. Resources and resource people can act as catalysts, offer an extra dimension and facilitate the functioning of the group, but the key part is the parents themselves. By sharing their own concerns and experience they will draw

strength from each other, recognise some of their own current skills, realise that they are not alone in the struggle to parent well and gain new insights to help them in their task. Hence it should be a highly interactive group. It can be very helpful if it is made up of a mixture of parents with and without a Christian faith. Christian parents need as much help and support in this area as anyone. By having a mixed group each will learn from the other, friendships will be formed and support mechanisms established which are likely to last long after the group itself has ceased to function.

2 The leader, therefore, needs to be skilled in handling group processes if the full value of the sessions is to be gained.

3 Ensure the child-care that was agreed in the planning is run to the highest standards so that all the parents can participate in the group without anxiety about their child.

4 Evaluate the course after each session so that any adjustments to content and style can be made as the course progresses. Then, at the close of the course, do a full and thorough evaluation in preparation for any ongoing group or for future courses.

Stop

Consider the possibility of running a parentcraft course based in your church family.

- Who do you need to consult?
- What action do you need to take?

Parentcraft courses of any type have a number of potential outcomes:

1 They help to develop family life within the church itself thus enabling the life of Christ to be more fully revealed through individual members and the community as a whole.

2 They place Christian and non-Christian alongside each other as equals. There should therefore be a learning process in both directions, opening the non-believer up to the truth of God and his ways and opening the believer to a better understanding of their neighbours and their lives.

3 They act as a support and development base for families and should therefore help with the growth of God's justice and righteousness being enacted in a neighbourhood.

4 They may highlight the need for an ongoing parent support group for at least some of those who have been on the course. This would fit into the wider area of family support which we look at in the next chapter.

Helping parents to be good enough parents (none are perfect!) is part of how God's people can fulfil the creation mandate to care for his earth and all that is in it. The rule of God is extended more fully as we seek to see his kingdom come as parents are made more conscious of God's role and activity in their lives and the life of their child(ren). Eventually they may even come to know and experience the loving parenthood of God for themselves.

Resources

CPAS Parenting Course: information from the Sales Office, Church Pastoral Aid Society, Athena Drive, Tachbrook Park, Warwick CV34 6NG; telephone Leamington Spa (0926) 334242, fax (0926) 337613.

The Veritas Trust organises regional workshops on parenting. Contact the Trust at 37 Balmoral Crescent, Dronfield

Woodhouse, Sheffield, Derbyshire S18 5ZY; telephone Chesterfield 410122.

Especially recommended are the **Family Caring Trust programmes**: available from Family Caring, 44 Rathfriland Road, Newry, County Down, BT34 1LD. These include:

Basic Parenting Programme
Teen Parenting Programme
Parenting and Sex Programme
Parent Assertiveness Programme

The James Dobson videos are widely used but a note of caution is warranted. They are simply lectures on video and are therefore not interactive, unless followed by discussion. Dobson frequently presents his views as if they are 'the biblical way'. In fact they are often closely aligned to the work and thinking of the behavioural psychologist B F Skinner. Skinner has some important and helpful insights into children's behaviour and development but he does not give much credence to the work of other psychologists such as Piaget, Donaldson, Bruner and Erickson. Seen in the light of their work, biblical texts can be understood in markedly different ways from those presented by Dobson. His work then can be well used, but not as the last and final word as it often seems to be presented. The videos are generally available in Christian bookshops.

8
FAMILY SUPPORT

Families are always under some degree of pressure, whatever their make-up and wherever individual members of them are within the Family Life Cycle. It is only reasonable, therefore, to assume that at all times families need a degree of support. This is acknowledged in the very structures of society, with the provision of financial support through state benefits such as child benefit and family credit, and the availability of family care centres, family therapists, and family advice through organisations like the Citizens Advice Bureau. Whether or not this provision is either adequate or the best is irrelevant here; my point is simply that the existence of these support mechanisms shows a need for family support. The followers of Jesus should not be surprised by this at all. The Bible is full of family support mechanisms and stories of family support.

For example, careful provisions were made for aliens, widows and orphans in Old Testament law. No one was to take unfair advantage of them; financial provision was to be made for them to ensure that they did not go hungry and were adequately clothed and housed (*cf* Deuteronomy 24 and the story of Ruth). Here is family support at work in very down to earth, practical ways.

Then note the seriousness with which God viewed Israel's failure to put this into action (Amos 2:6–7; 4:1–3; 5:11–15; Isaiah 1:17, 23; 10:12; Jeremiah 7:5–8; Ezekiel 16:49. Note here that Sodom's sin was her arrogance and failure to care for the needy). The New Testament affirms that the standards for God's ancient people Israel were to be those of the new Israel as well, except that the new Israel was to live by the spirit of the law rather than merely by its letter (*cf* Matthew 5–7; Acts 2:42–47; 4:32–35; 6:1–2; James 1:27; 1 John 3:11ff).

Jesus supported his own family through his work as a carpenter until his younger brothers and sisters were able to care for themselves. He cared for other families too (Matthew 8:5–13; Matthew 9:18–26; Matthew 15:21–28; Luke 7:11ff; Luke 10:38–42; John 11: 1–44; Luke 17:11–15).

So offering support to families in their various needs is part and parcel of God's calling to his people. What needs to be done is to identify the areas where support is needed today and for local churches to develop ways in which they can be part of responding to those needs. What follows are some suggested areas. But these are not intended to be exhaustive. In every locality, careful prayer and thought needs to be given to the areas of need that exist and appropriate action then taken.

Parent Support Groups

The purpose of this type of group is not primarily to look at parenting skills as happens in parentcraft courses. The focus rather is on mutual support and encouragement. It is simply a time and place for parents to meet and openly share their concerns with one another. The group may meet weekly, fortnightly or monthly and will centre on being a self-help group which may need a convenor and facilitator who is not one of the parents, but who recognises the need to meet for this support. In order for it to act as a support group rather than simply a place to drink coffee together, a certain minimal amount of structure and direction might be needed as might child care. (If all the children were at nursery, playgroup or school, such a group might be able to meet during school hours, though this is likely to exclude working parents and probably, therefore, fathers in particular.)

This type of group may arise out of the expressed needs in a parentcraft course or may be established independently. In some instances it may actually precede parentcraft. Some parents may be put off by the parentcraft model as 'not for me', but may value a more informal group like the one envisaged in this section. In whatever way such a group comes into being, and however it actually functions, it can be an enormous encouragement to those who take part. (At times it may be appropriate for the group to be mothers only or fathers only because of particular circumstances associated with individuals in the group.) A mixed group of Christians and non-Christians would be most effective in helping both groups grasp their common human needs and something of the difference that Christ can make in a family.

Family Support
Parents have a great deal to offer and to learn. Parentcraft and parent support groups will help with this. However, wider support than this may be needed.

Home Support
When a new baby is born the State recognises the need to give support through a midwife, a doctor, maternity leave, health visitors and maternity benefit. Yet why do so many local churches appear to assume that since the State is busy providing all of this they need do nothing? Surely a sensitive level of care can be offered by people of all ages and statuses in the church. A little co-ordination will help to ensure that the family is not overwhelmed by offers one day, whilst left unaided the next. We have become far too insular and self-dependent in Western societies thinking that to ask for or need help is a sign of weakness and

failure. Such a view is wrong. A single parent needs a break from time to time for her own sanity and personal health. A couple need time together to talk, enjoy being together, make love without fear of interruption by a baby or child. This kind of support can be given by anyone – single people, young or old, other families with children or childless couples. And it is never a one-way process. As they are giving space to others carers will be gaining much themselves.

The need for support does not diminish as children grow older. It changes its nature as the particular needs of both children and parents change with age and development.

Now in many churches some of this does happen and is extremely good. However, it is often confined within the circle of the church. People outside can have a much smaller network of support around them than exists within the church community. Surely churches should be far more outward-looking in offering help out of a concern for the welfare of their neighbours' lives. As they do so, it will have an impact for the good news of Jesus as God's love is put into action.

This should be happening spontaneously, but there is also a place for a church to organise a strong pastoral support network, with visitors, carers, willing cooks, babysitters, and so forth, all known about and ready to be called upon as and when a need arises.

Parent and Toddler, Play and Nursery Groups

Large numbers of churches have developed groups like these in recent years. (For example, 871 Baptist churches in England, Wales and Scotland run parent and toddler groups, and 434 run playgroups. This is out of a total of 1,972 Baptist congregations [Figures from *Baptist Times*, 4 November 1993]). They do an invaluable work of service to the community and act as a clear link between the church community and the local community within which it is set. Any groups like these must be run to the highest possible standards. They need to comply with any relevant legislation covering the running of such groups (eg The Children Act 1989 for England and Wales).

By their very nature these groups act as support to families through high quality child care. They often act as a focus for the development of friendships between parents from church and non-church backgrounds.

After School and Children's Clubs
These are often run primarily for the benefit of the children. (The Baptist statistics show 121 after school groups and 337 other children's groups being run in the 1,972 churches. This excludes Sunday schools which run in nearly all the churches.) This clearly has validity, but if it is the only reasoning behind the running of them, then I would suggest that some more thinking is needed.

Many parents today have to work and need care for their children after school through childminding or clubs. For a local church or church members to provide these services is to fulfil a much broader function than simply offering the children something interesting to do. They actually function as a means of support to that family unit as it seeks to hold itself together and develop. Children need adequate peer group activity and the influence and support of adult role models outside of the home as they grow and develop, and such groups provide these.

I am convinced that groups like these, and more traditional groups such as Sunday schools, need to be seen in this broader context. To operate groups like these in isolation from the overall structure and strategy of the local church community is to operate with an inadequate model of the whole life of the church community and to restrict the range of family support that we offer. As to the actual running of these clubs I described this more fully in an earlier book, *Reaching Children*.

The need for this support continues on into the teenage years when the importance of the peer group and adult role models/confidants outside of the immediate family grows even greater. The 'youth club' and 'youth work', however it is structured, should form part of the overall life of the church community as it seeks to serve and reach out into its local community, contributing to the development of future family life as young people work out their personality, sexuality, lifestyles and skills. It will at times be a period of overlap. For example, the teenager who has a baby will need to be offered ongoing support: as a young person; as a family member handling the reactions of parents, grandparents and siblings; and as a new parent herself. Perhaps this example highlights the reality that family support is an ongoing process, which involves people at every phase of their lives.

Families with special needs

Some families have individuals within them who are classified as having 'special needs'. Often this is only thought of with reference to children but this should not be the case. A family may have a child with Down's syndrome, a young adult with multiple sclerosis, an ageing family member with Alzheimer's disease, or some other specific need. Such family members may live in the same household, or independently, or in an institution or care facility. Whatever the specific 'need' and family structure, the existence of such individuals within a family creates extra pressures which, in turn, give rise to additional support requirements.

The local church community ought to make itself aware of the ways it could offer support to these families, just as with the other areas of need noted earlier in the chapter. Should it, for example, seriously consider running a group for people with learning difficulties? Or find ways of providing respite care for the carers? Or should it ensure that

Family support

some of its members are trained in deaf signing or Makoton signing to enable greater accessibility for people with these specific needs? No doubt it will not be possible for any one local congregation to provide support in every direction. But with careful co-operation a group of churches could ensure a very wide breadth of provision, and many in that local community might think again about the relevance of the church and of its message of God's love for all people.

Stop

- What support do families in your church and local community need?
- What support is already being offered?
- What changes could be made to enhance the level of support offered particularly to those outside the church community?

Grandparenting

In days of yore, grandparents were key players in family support structures. In many societies they remain so, as indeed they still do in Western societies particularly amongst many of the smaller ethnic groups. Grandparents bring all their parenting experience to bear as guides, mentors, supporters and carers. With the geographical distance which so often separates grandparents from their grandchildren in the modern world their role has decreased. This has been further exacerbated by the rapid change in society. In previous eras the world of parents and grandparents was not vastly different. However, with the Industrial Revolution, the technological revolution, advances in transportation and changing patterns of employment – the two worlds are often very far apart. Thus the wisdom of the elderly tends to be regarded as rather old-fashioned and irrelevant to the needs of modern family life. There may be some truth in this, but this is only a partial truth. The elderly still have a great deal of wisdom and experience which is relevant and needed when it comes to caring for children. Often a teenager will confide in a grandparent in a way in which they cannot/will not with a parent. The grandparent may have time and space to look after a young child whilst the parent goes out shopping or to work. In particular this supportive role can be crucial where the parent is alone or where economically both parents need to work.

Joan was in her late fifties when her eldest daughter's marriage broke up. Maureen (the daughter) found that she needed to go out to work, but she could not find a job which paid her enough to cover the cost of child care. So Joan arranged to change her working hours so that she was finished by the close of school. Maureen took responsibility for the boys in the morning, but Grandma Joan was there when they returned home from school and produced the evening meal. She also 'baby-sat' on occasions so that Maureen could have an evening out with her new man. Joan took the boys along to some church activities because they enjoyed them and Mum never quite made the effort to get them there. Over the years, Grandma Joan was the one who actually offered the boys their greatest security. They were well-loved by their mum, and cared for, but somehow they could talk to Grandma more openly, and she was always there when they needed her.

Grandparents may be too far away to provide such support for their own grandchildren, but they could act as surrogate grandparents for a family more local to them. Or perhaps there is an elderly person who is single or a couple who never had children of their own. Again this has a two-way benefit: elderly people get a chance to care and love, helping them to maintain their own sense of worth and purpose in a world where they are so often devalued.

This all has to be born in mind when a church is considering what resources it can offer by way of care and carers for family support. It may mean that training needs to be organised for such 'grandparents' to help them realise their skills and to develop new ones. Such a role will never be without its difficulties and tensions. Communication between parent and 'grandparent' will need to be clear so that agreed patterns of care are developed and adhered to. The possible gains for all involved are enormous.

Stop

What human resources for grandparenting do you have in your church community? How can these be released into action?

It will be clear from the last two chapters that the local church community has a great deal to offer a wide range of families through parentcraft training, parent and family support and grandparenting. These are all ways of seeking the wholeness of a local community and of the family units within it. They are not 'evangelistic' in any traditional sense of the word because they are run as appropriate in their own terms. However, their impact in communicating the good news to people of all ages can be immense. We fail to use them to the detriment of the kingdom of God.

Resources

Happy Birthday Anyway, A Study Guide to Ageing, Joan King, Church House Publishing, 1990.

Young Adult Programme from *Family Caring Trust* (see 'Resources', Chapter 7).

Causeway is part of 'A Cause for Concern' and, among other things, exists to encourage the setting up and running of Bible groups for people with mental handicaps. Further information from: A Cause For Concern, PO Box 351, Reading, RG1 7AL.

We're All Special To God, David and Madeleine Potter, Scripture Union, 1990.

DIY Training Course: *The Local Church and People with Mental Handicaps*, from Scripture Union Training Unit, 26–30 Heathcoat Street, Nottingham NG1 3AA; telephone Nottingham (0602) 418144, fax (0602) 414624.

Resource people

Scripture Union's Family Adviser, contact Scripture Union at the Nottingham address (see above).

Family Life and Marriage Education (FLAME) at 11 Mundy Street, Heanor, Derbyshire DE75 7EB; telephone Langley Mill (0733) 761579.

The Mothers' Union, The Mary Sumner House, 24 Tufton Street, London SW1P 3RB; telephone 0171-222 5533.

The Children's Society, Edward Rudolph House, 69 Margery Street, London WC1X 0JL; telephone 0171-837 4299.

Dr Barnados, Tanners Lane, Barkingside, Ilford, Essex; telephone 0181-550 8822.

Denominational Advisers

9

FAMILY TO FAMILY

Whilst it has been proposed in previous chapters that visiting is a crucial part of pastoral care, there are other ways that families can be reached. Presenting people with the large task of reaching the families in their area may seem too ambitious for many. But supposing each family unit sought to reach one or two others by befriending and caring. Suddenly the task becomes more manageable.

The suggestion is quite straightforward: a Christian family befriends, prays for and shares the life of Christ with one or two other families. These families could be the next door neighbours, or perhaps a family with children at the same school. Natural ties like those made at the school gate, playgroup or leisure activity should be taken up. But there ought also to be an openness to befriending a family whose situation and make-up is different. Perhaps there is an elderly couple whose family live a long way away and who rarely see their grandchildren of a similar age to the children in the Christian family. A friendship built could be socially beneficial in both directions. Or maybe a Christian who is a single parent with one child will befriend a family where both parents are at home. The friendship could provide peer group friendships for the children; a male role model; alternative models of parenting for each family and mutual support whenever it is needed.

Such building of relationships between families can

create natural opportunities for sharing the good news. It also places the Christians in a position where they become aware of the needs of another family. It creates the opportunity for the non-believers to serve and care for the believers. If it truly is 'more blessed to give than receive' why do we spend so much time suggesting that for non-believers to be blessed they must always receive from us? Surely as we allow them to give of themselves – to care and love their neighbours – they will find real blessing and release? In this very process, they may realise more of what it means to be truly human. They will be discovering something of the image of God within them. This may be one way that the Spirit of God actually breaks through into their lives.

Whilst wanting to see the life of the believing community built up through Christians simply being together, time must always be available for believers to spend with those outside the kingdom. Going swimming as families, having picnics out, watching a video together, going to a sports game or the cinema or pantomime, helping each other with gardening or decorating; almost anything to do with simply living and seeking to make the most of life. Christians thus expose their faith to the scrutiny of others. They put themselves in positions where life and life's issues are bound to crop up in conversation and they can simply share what they perceive to be the Christian view.

As lives are shared like this, naturally and openly, so it becomes easier to pray for the family and its needs. When things like parenting or family support groups are established, invitations can be given in the context of genuine friendship. Non-believers will understand that such a group is not likely to be too threatening, especially if they can go with their Christian friends. Invitations to more evangelistic events are more likely to be accepted because of the trust and care that has been established between the two families and the individuals within them.

Some Christian homes can be places of relaxation and refuge for adolescents struggling with relating to their parents. Here the thought is not particularly about teenagers facing major traumas, though they are included; it is more about the average teenager who needs an adult outside of the home whom they can trust and with whom they can talk. If families have developed an ongoing relationship over a period of years, a teenager from a non-Christian background might well look to and confide in a Christian adult. This person may be a youth leader, but they may just be a friend. (It can also work the other way around with a teenager from a Christian background confiding in a non-believing adult.)

What is needed in this context is time, a listening ear, occasional words of wisdom, plenty of coffee and cake. I can personally remember hundreds of hours spent as a teenager in the kitchen of a neighbour eating tons of chocolate cake and drinking gallons of coffee! This was immensely valuable – a place to be away from the parents, and the opportunity to talk about life, the universe and everything. There were heated discussions, open disagreements and mutual learning which just never seemed quite possible with the parents with whom I always had a very good relationship. It was a part of one family reaching another.

Another aspect of this family-befriending-family is the wider family context it can offer to someone living on their own. A single person has a family but they may be a long way away. He or she might value having a family to be welcomed into and to 'become a part of'. They may have nephews and nieces who they rarely see and would be glad of some time with children in a similar family setting. Or they may not. Each person has their own preferences. Still the offer of friendship and welcome should be there. (There is of course no reason why the initiative for such an openness should not be taken by the single person towards a neighbouring family.)

Families Exploring the Gospel Together

On some occasions these family-to-family relationships may take on a more overtly evangelistic nature. So often when it comes to specific evangelism the family is divided up into children, young people, women and men. The men are invited to men's breakfasts or suppers; the women to similar meals or coffee mornings; the young people to evangelistic concerts or drama; the children to a holiday club. Now all of these are perfectly valid and good, but do we always have to divide families up into these homogeneous groups?

There is potential for evangelism in setting up ways for a couple of families to explore the good news together in their own homes. A family with Christians in it, having established good friendships, could suggest to another family that they get together perhaps once a week for two to three weeks to explore the Christian faith together. It must be done with an openness to the possibility of the Christians learning from the non-Christians; not with a sense of 'We're going to give it to you now'. Here are two ways in which this might work:

1 Watching a film or video together

The families might agree to watch a film together and then talk about its content. Suitable films could include *Chariots of Fire*, *The Tanglewoods' Secret* or *Bledlow Range*. They need not necessarily be such overtly Christian stories though. *Sister Act*, *The Mission*, *Twins* or *Leap of Faith* are all examples of films which can create plenty of discussion. The particular film would need to be appropriate to the age of any children watching. (The post-film discussion should obviously include the children/young people.) It may be that a full length film is split into two parts with viewing and discussion after each, separated by a week. However, this can be very frustrating for the viewer, so an alternative would be to view the film through completely one week and discuss it the following one. One of the glories of video is the possibility of rewinding and replaying at ease. So if it will help the discussion or clarify a disagreement, relevant scenes can be replayed during the discussion.

Another alternative would be to use a shorter video like those produced by Scripture Union or one of the *McGee and Me* stories. The post-viewing activity need not be discussion. Why not do some family role plays or produce some art work? Suggestions for activities are always included with Scripture Union's videos, so the work, in this instance, will already have been done.

2 Reading the Bible together

Another idea would be to agree to look at the story of Jesus together. Time would be spent reading a story from the Gospels and discovering together what it is all about, using atlases, dictionaries and other suitable reference books, then sharing what the story means to each person involved. This would then be followed by doing something creative to express what has been learnt or talked about.

This is essentially an adaptation of the ideas presented by Walter Wink in *Transforming Bible Study* and Patricia van Ness in *Transforming Bible Study with Children*. The heart of this method is to have an openness to the insights that everyone gains from the text. It is a shared approach which builds on the relationship base of family-to-family. The very methods involved should further and deepen the existing relationships. The accent is definitely on 'discovering together' rather than 'presenting to'; and it operates on the conviction that most people come to Christian faith through a gradual process rather than a sudden crisis.

It would be unlikely that such an activity would last for

more than two or three weeks. But it is likely that if things have gone well then it would bear repeating a few months later. Initially a 'one off' session would probably be best; but at the end of that, all involved may want to repeat it. Perhaps a once a month or every two months pattern would be even better.

Incidentally this might be the only time when the Christian family actually explore the Bible together as well.

Conclusions

Whatever the particular structure of a family in a particular locality, the possibility and potential of one family unit befriending another is enormous. It is an aspect of hospitality and offering welcome to those outside the kingdom which is not taken up enough in most local church settings. Often so much time can be used up on the internal life of a church, that it is impossible to give adequate time to developing outside relationships. This needs to change. One family reaching another with the gospel through relationship, natural openings and in creative time spent exploring the good news together must be one way forward for the spreading of the gospel in our day.

Stop

Consider the ideas in this chapter.

- What do you make of them?
- How could you and your family try one out?

Resources

Family Evangelism, John Hattam, can be obtained from the Scripture Union Missions Department, 130 City Road, London EC1V 2NJ.

Transforming Bible Study, Walter Wink, Mowbray, 1990.

Transforming Bible Study with Children, Patricia van Ness, Abingdon (US), 1991.

International Films – productions are available through Scripture Press (see below).

Videos can be obtained from:

Scripture Union Mail Order, 9–11 Clothier Road, Bristol BS4 5RL; telephone 0117–9719709, fax 0117–9711472.

Scripture Press Foundation (UK) Ltd, Raans Road, Amersham, Buckinghamshire HP6 6JQ; telephone Amersham (0494) 722151, fax (0494) 726607.

10
GETTING AWAY FROM IT ALL

Imagine a single parent household which consists of Mum, four children aged from three to eleven, living in a high-rise block of flats on the third floor. Father comes to stay occasionally, but always arrives unannounced and departs without warning. Grandmother lives with the family for at least six months of the year. She is wheelchair-bound and has to use a commode. The lifts in the block work on average two days a week. The only income is State benefits. The mother 'failed' at school because she had her first child at sixteen and spent much of her final school year feeling sick, being heavily pregnant and adapting to motherhood. She is now trying to study to retake some of the exams she was well capable of passing but failed.

This is not imagination, but a true situation. Imagine the stresses and strains which build up within this household. Imagine some of the things said in the midst of that tension. How could you ever get away from it all?

Or imagine a single woman in her seventies living alone in her flat on the top floor of a Victorian house. Her income is a State pension plus a small occupational one. She is increasingly frail and needs the support of home helps, meals-on-wheels and other agencies. She has now become too frail to climb down the stairs on her own. She never married. She has no children or grandchildren. Her only living relatives live several hundred miles away and only remember her at Christmas. Imagine how lonely she has become, her feelings and the questions. This too is a true situation. How could you get away from it all?

An answer for both the households described has been through the creative work of Christian groups getting these people 'away from it all' for at least a few days. The impact on all involved was considerable. For the distressed young mother – laughter, relaxation and enjoyment; a sense of being able to go back to the regular pattern of life with renewed energies and a fresh sense of support from others around her. The children discovered new abilities, experienced new things, found new friends. Grandmother enjoyed her respite care so much that she thought that perhaps she would like to experience it again after all. For the elderly single lady – having someone to talk to whenever she felt like it; being taken out to see the sights; being left alone to watch the waves break on the shore and recalling happy memories of her childhood; enjoying the sight and sound of young children playing around her; enjoying good food (the meals-on-wheels were fine, but they became rather tedious sometimes!).

Although returning home prompted mixed feelings for them all, it was 'home' and appreciated a little more for having been away for a while. There were good memories to ponder, new relationships made and the prospect of another chance to get away from it all next year, if not before. And in the midst of it all had come an awareness of the reality of God. The Christians accompanying them were far from perfect; they had lost their tempers, not always been polite, not always treated others with respect and yet there was something about them which rang true. God seemed real to them. Jesus made some kind of a difference to them as individuals and in the way they related to each other. It was certainly worth thinking about some more . . .

It would be possible to tell stories of people who actually professed Christian commitment on 'family holidays', but more often, for someone going away like this, it will simply be a part of a longer process.

The Weekend Break

Many churches have established a pattern of a church weekend away, perhaps every year or two. Often the focus of these is 'teaching' with an outside speaker taking sessions for the adults whilst people from the church, or possibly from a neighbouring church or outside organisation, come along and run a separate programme for the children and young people. The focus, it has to be admitted, tends to be on existing church members and, in particular, on the adults. If anyone from outside the regular life of the church came along they would more often than not drop out of the sessions because they were too 'heavy'.

No doubt there is some validity in these weekends. (I must think so as I have spoken at enough of them!) But I want to suggest that with more thought and adaptation, such weekend breaks can actually be a very powerful way of helping people outside the life of the church to experience more of the community life of God's family and be drawn to Christ through it.

Let's forget 'the outsider' for a moment. Weekends away can be very powerful tools for developing and nurturing the community life of the church, and when we are being honest we have to admit that many churches actually have very little real sense of community. It is quite possible to structure these weekends in such a way that all ages enjoy each other's company, learn and worship together and experience something more of being family, both as a family unit and as an extended family together.

First, a double shift in focus is needed. The focus must be more on *being together* rather than on *teaching*. Second, the focus must be on *all ages together* rather than *adults only*. Some immediately shy away because they feel the teaching element is so crucial and/or because they cannot imagine how 'all ages together' can actually work.

The question of *teaching* really poses the question of *learning*. You can import the best Bible teacher in the country to speak at a weekend and many will probably go away saying how wonderful the talks were. But what will they actually have *learnt* about God, themselves and one another? Without a depth of experience together, and without the opportunity to reflect and formulate fresh ideas and thoughts for action, there will have been no real learning. To arrange a weekend so that people have time to be together and do things together, and to give them scope within that to reflect, will actually lead to a deeper learning experience which will last beyond nice feelings about a good speaker.

Then the question of 'all ages' raises a very serious underlying problem. If all ages cannot spend time together, do things together, reflect on things together and share their learning from it, then there is zero hope for any family life at all. People in families are having to live and share with people of all ages continually. So if it can and does happen on a small scale it must be possible for it to happen on the larger scale. It is not that it cannot work; it is rather that it has not been tried or betrays a deep underlying problem that adults have in relating to children at all. (The problem is usually that way around, though not always.)

Stop

Consider the points made about teaching/learning and 'all ages together'.

- What are your honest thoughts and feelings about this?

Hannah and her brother Pete excitedly held up their group collage. A group of fifteen made up of all ages had been out in the woods collecting moss, twigs, leaves, soil, scraps of paper, almost anything they could find. Then together they had talked about 'our church' and had created a picture out of all these natural elements to express their feelings about 'our church' which they then shared with three other groups who were doing something similar. Hannah spoke up for the group. 'It was brill! I've never done anything with old people in the church before and it was great fun.' The smiles on the faces of everyone else told the story even more eloquently. By the time all four groups had shared their very varied pictures, there was a deep sense of gratitude to God. 'We'll never quite see our church in the same way again,' Hazel, one of the church leaders, said. 'I never realised that the children had so much to contribute.' 'And I'd never realised you could be such fun,' ten year old Marcia piped up happily. The whole room laughed and then broke into a song of praise. It was one of those moments when you knew God had done something to build his people together.

To illustrate how such weekend breaks can be run, a couple of sample programmes and timetables follow. They show two possibilities. In the first, although the overall programme is integrated, it contains a mixture of all-age *and* peer group sessions. In the other, the whole programme is integrated. Within each session the focus is on *being and learning together* just as it is for the whole weekend. The other key matter here is the venue. If the focus is on being and doing things together this is obviously easier to do if the venue has appropriate facilities and/or is within easy reach of these.

Reaching families

Programme One

FRIDAY
Late afternoon/early evening: Arrival, evening meal.
Evening: A 'light' all-age session for anyone who is awake and about. It introduces the theme of the weekend and includes fun activities.

SATURDAY
After breakfast: Adults, young people and children meet separately, but all the sessions are around the same theme and feed into the all-together session in the second half of the morning.
After mid-morning break: All together exploring a new aspect of the theme, but with time and scope for sharing together what has been covered in the separate groups.
Afternoon: Free, but could include some organised games/activities for people of all ages to join in.
Evening: A fun all-age event or activity.

SUNDAY
After breakfast: As Saturday morning and with time to reflect back over Friday and Saturday.
After mid-morning break: All together. Again, include input from earlier session and perhaps communion.
Afternoon: Enjoy each other's company again in a variety of activities.

The order of the Sunday 'after mid-morning' and Sunday afternoon sessions could be reversed.

Programme Two

FRIDAY
Late afternoon/early evening: Arrival, evening meal.
Evening: An all-age activity starting as early as practicable, to set the tone and theme for the weekend.

SATURDAY

Morning: All-age workshops with time to share together from these.
Afternoon: A range of outings and activities available for people to choose from. These should all be suitable for all ages. Individuals or family groups may want free time to go and do their own thing.
Evening: A family film, concert or barn dance.

SUNDAY
Morning: Re-run the Saturday morning workshops, giving people a chance to do one they didn't do previously, or put on a new selection.
Conclusion: Close the weekend with some all-age worship either before or after lunch.

Within either style of programme you may want to form some small 'family' groups. These would consist of a mixture of household types, so that you may have a husband and wife with their three small children, a widow, a single parent with teenage daughter, a lone teenager, a single adult in their thirties, and an elderly couple – all in one group. These can act as 'base groups' to which, from time to time in the programme, everyone returns for sharing, reflection, prayer or whatever. These would need to be worked out before people arrive or during the first evening, and time should be given on that first evening for them to get together. The groups act as a microcosm of the whole and a stable social factor for everyone.

You may find it necessary to have some form of crèche running for the smallest children (up to about the age of three) during most of the activities. But involve even these smaller children wherever possible, even if only for short periods of time.

Some readers probably remain sceptical about this type of weekend. Isn't it rather lightweight spiritually? The answer is a straightforward 'NO' and that is based on my experience of these weekends and on the testimony of many others who have been involved with them. Sceptics have regularly been 'converted' by the accessibility and appeal of such weekends to non-churchgoers; the amount of learning that actually happened; the sheer fun; and the real awareness of God's presence in and through it all.

Longer Holidays

The essential principles are clearly the same. It is about *being together*. The use of family base groups can again be very valuable as can all-age workshops, games, worship and the like. The programme should not be too 'heavy', if it is really meant to be a holiday which non-church people will want to join in with and feel part of.

Brief children's and young people's sessions straight after breakfast may be valuable whilst adults are getting everything ready for the day out. Otherwise an all-age learning and worship session in the early evening would be the only other obvious 'spiritual' input to include. This clearly needs to be very relaxed, with a holiday feel; but that does not mean it has to be any less serious or meaningful. Time and again people say how valuable and significant these kinds of sessions have been to them. The days need to be left free for everyone to go off to the beach, sightsee, walk or do whatever they fancy. But because people of all ages from all sorts of households are taking part there ought to be continual offers of doing things together, creating different family and social groupings from day to day.

An individual church may find it a struggle to run such a holiday on its own, so joining with another church or two from the area or even further afield might be a solution.

Such holidays can be run by taking over a boarding school or college premises, making a block booking at a hotel, camping, taking several caravans on one site, or

Getting away from it all

going to a conference centre. They can be for just a few people or for a large group; in Britain or on the continent; for five days or a fortnight. Or they could involve going as a group to a larger organised 'family' holiday arranged by one of the Christian organisations or conference centres. (Though if you are keen to encourage non-believers to be part of your group ensure they will feel comfortable with this.) The range of possibilities for such holidays is large. It is the will to plan them that is usually the biggest obstacle to be overcome.

The Brixton Family Weeks all began in the hearts and minds of two wonderful West Indian ladies. They were in contact with a number of families in need. Some of these families were involved with a local church, others were not. Several were single parent households, but not all. The common factor was that each family was under pressure. None of them could ever get away from their homes because finances were just too tight. Tiredness built up in a big way. 'Can you help us take them away for a few days to give them a break?' was the request that came to two of us working in Scripture Union. It would be a big task because we would have to find a suitable venue, a team who could arrange activities for the children for some of the time, to allow the mums space to 'be' and to talk and simply to go to the shops without a baby buggy.

The first year was not a roaring success. The venue failed to give adequate privacy, was too noisy, too cut off from the rest of civilisation and the food was done on too tight a budget. But the lessons were heeded and it was seen as a good enough start to try again. The next time the 'mums' were given a much greater say in the style of programme, the venue was changed and we made sure that the food was really good (this was, after all, their only holiday of the year). As the week passed, you could see the tension easing from some of the parents. They became more relaxed, laughed more, even responded to their children differently. The same was true of the children; some learnt how to relate to other children and other adults in ways they had never been able to do before. Some realised that male adults could be fun and could be trusted. Others simply had a great time. It was hard work for the team: up very early and to bed very late; changing activities, it seemed, every five minutes because some of the children had such low concentration levels; discovering a love for the children, and sometimes, unexpectedly receiving loving responses from them. God was seen to be at work, bringing a greater sense of wholeness to everyone who took part.

Personally I learned a lot from the week. Being one of the very few adult males with around twenty women creates an interesting situation. Being one of only three white people amongst fifty Afro-Caribbeans also highlights lessons about racial prejudice, stereotyping and the like. The Christmas party reunions each year were hilarious and chaotic. Hearing about the ongoing love and support given to the families by local Christians made it clear that the holidays were only part of a wider work in which commitment to community and care was very high. I always felt that I learnt far more from this group than I ever gave. If anyone has taught me that being 'family' as Christians is possible, exciting and powerful, then it has been these people. This white, middle class male thanks God for black working women and children who gave him both vision and experience of 'family' he had never experienced elsewhere.

Whatever style of 'getting away from it all' is chosen decisions have to be made. The key decision is the principle. Turning that into practice will involve a range of practical factors such as the length, venue, style, clientele, dates and a host of nitty-gritty issues like budgets and transport.

Practical Factors to Consider

Budget
The cost per person and per family will obviously be crucial. Taking a whole household away can be very expensive so keep an eye on the overall costs. Consider creating a fund to help those on low incomes/with large families. You may even find you can get grants from local authorities and charities to help some people. If you don't ask you don't receive! Experience has shown that sometimes the supposedly 'anti-Christian' local authority will come up with a very substantial grant, whilst a Christian charity might not be able to help.

Accommodation
What kind is available? Is it suitable for the hoped-for clientele? Is it possible to offer a range of types of accommodation? What other facilities are available for games/leisure activities, either on site or in the near vicinity?

Food
Will the holiday be self-catering or catered for? Can special diets be accommodated? Will the food be plentiful and of good quality? (Poor food has spoilt many holidays which have been good in all other respects.)

Transport
How will everyone get there? How will they move around once they have arrived? What cars are available? Might a minibus or two be useful for taking several people together, and for use during the holiday. Does a coach offer less flexibility? Do you have adequately qualified drivers for minibuses?

Reaching families

Insurance
Is adequate insurance available for any personal injuries on the holiday or any public liability involved? And can you run to some kind of cancellation insurance scheme? If people are paying for the transport, are car/minibus drivers and owners operating within the limits of their insurances?

Special Needs
It's great to be able to take people with special needs on these holidays. But if they are in a wheelchair, is access suitable? If they are incontinent, are commodes, laundry facilities etc available? Are you ready to integrate special needs people into your programme and sessions? The list obviously goes on. These are not reasons to exclude special needs people from the holiday, but they are issues to consider in choosing a venue, types of activity, transport and so forth. If you cannot accommodate special needs at a particular venue, go somewhere where you can!

Timing
When is the best time for the holiday for the people coming? How long should it be?

Programme
What kind of programme would you envisage running? Who will organise this and take responsibility for it actually happening? What plans need to be made for the vagaries of the weather, people's tastes and the availability of facilities?

Planning a weekend or holiday break is a lot of work and has to be done well in advance. But such are the benefits of these kinds of breaks, that all the hard work is worth it in the end. Whilst away, whether it be for a brief weekend or longer, the people who go create a temporary community. Within that they experience fresh insights into family and community life; they have the opportunity to establish new friendships, or deepen existing ones; they make new discoveries about others and themselves. Where this temporary community includes those who love God and seek to serve him, and where some opportunity is given to allow the loving presence and power of 'Father God' to move amongst the participants, the whole experience can be deeply significant. To be part of such a temporary community can enhance the well-being and wholeness of all who take part, not simply for the time spent away but in the longer term, as the stories at the beginning of the chapter illustrated. Finally, to belong to such a temporary community can be the means by which some enter the kingdom of heaven because, however imperfectly, they have experienced it for themselves.

Stop

Spend a short while thinking about a time when you have been away with a group of other people.

- What was its value for you?
- Are there people outside your church who may be interested in 'getting away from it all'?
- What plans could you make to bring this about?

Further Reading

The Temporary Community, Tom Slater; can be obtained from Scripture Union, 393 Smith Street, Fitzroy, Victoria 3065, Australia.

The Bumper Book of Family Activities, John Marshall, Scripture Union, 1994.

Signposts, Peter Privett, Church House Publishing, 1993.

11
'ONE OFF' FAMILY EVENTS

It will be abundantly clear by now that family evangelism is about an overall way of 'being the church'. It is about a commitment to the life of God's family people as a fundamental way of expressing the good news of Jesus. It is about finding and developing ways of helping families, whatever their circumstances and make-up, towards greater wholeness. And it is about sharing the love of God in and through the ongoing realities of life, rather than just another way of running specifically evangelistic events. Within this overall framework, however, there is a valid and proper place for specific events for families which are intended to be evangelistic in nature.

It is becoming quite common for holiday clubs aimed generally at primary age children to have within them a family event. These tend to be reasonably low-key in evangelistic terms. They may take the form of a barn dance or a family fun games evening. A family beetle drive has been known to work well too. Food and music also go down well. There can be a place for a good Christian video or an interview testimony within the context of the programme. A heavy evangelistic address would, however, be inappropriate in this setting.

But such events need not necessarily be linked to something like a holiday club. Within the church's overall planned strategy and programme there must be a place for 'family' evenings, days or even weekends. They can range from being primarily about fun and enjoyment, through being and doing things together, to being quite specifically evangelistic. (The latter should not be un-enjoyable though!)

A Broad Range of Possibilities
The range of such 'one off' events is becoming broader as more churches experiment with different possibilities.

Family fun night
Include plenty of simple team games played in 'family' groups each made up of around ten people from a variety of families and ages. If you struggle with getting men along to these, ask some of them to run a game rather than play as part of a team. They may prefer this role. Keep the whole evening moving and make sure that the games can be played by the youngest to the oldest and vary in the kinds of skills required. Built into such evenings can be some corporate craft activity and co-operative games like those played with parachutes (or play canopies).

Family quiz night
Once again teams should be made up from a variety of ages and family backgrounds. A series of rounds of questions should be well prepared. Having teams drawn from a wide age-range allows for a very broad scope in the questions. TV rounds can include children's programmes. Music can include the latest pop, classical music, and hits from the past and from musicals and films. Picture rounds can have the latest sporting heroines alongside ageing politicians or old time movie stars. The emphasis for such an evening should be on the fun and enjoyment of being involved. Family quiz nights are not intended to imitate the highly competitive nature of some quiz teams who play regularly in quiz leagues. Take great care that no one is left feeling

that they know nothing. Be prepared to include things which burst the bubble of arrogant pomposity if necessary.

Family workshop evening
Invite people to come along and learn a new skill. These could include simple bicycle maintenance; how to wire a plug; using a computer for beginners; cake decorating; cooking; gardening tips; learning to paint in watercolours; and, of course, many more are possible. It is surprising how wiring a plug for the first time can bring a sense of achievement, or learning to make marzipan flowers with which to decorate a cake. The options need to be skills that can be learnt and practised in an evening. Some might even be brief enough to allow people to try two new skills in an evening. The other important factor is to ensure that the people who are teaching the skill are competent to teach it as well as able to do it themselves. There is absolutely no need for the people leading the different skills groups to be Christians; they are there to help people learn a skill. The communication of God's good news should be coming through the whole event, by the way the Christians present relate to others and in any more specifically evangelistic presentation built into the evening.

Family treasure hunt
This can be set in the local area and involves the solving of clues, the finding out of information, doing it all as speedily as possible, and concluding with refreshments and entertainment once all the teams have returned.

Family video event
Each family group has a video camera and has to create their own story. An evening would be rather short for this, but a series of evenings or a whole day would make this feasible. Creating the storyboards, determining individual roles within the group, and producing it could

create a few moments of tension, but also make for a highly enjoyable event. The final grand showing of a number of such videos would bring lots of laughter if nothing else.

Barn dances

These are marvellous events for people of all ages to join in and mix together. A live band is preferable, but it is perfectly possible for dances to be run by a caller using records or tapes. A family disco might also be enjoyed by people from a very wide age range. These can draw on pop music from a wide era or they can be run as theme nights. A theme night allows people the fun of dressing appropriately in '50s, '60s, '70s or '80s gear. The music should obviously tie in with the era. Do make sure that with any type of dance event there is plenty of refreshment around.

The thrust of all such events should be on building relationships. It needs to be made clear that they are open to people who are single, have no children, grandparents, and from any ethnic background as well. This demands clear publicity and the use of 'family groups' constituted especially for the event (meeting, for example, around a quiz table or in a video-making team), rather than using nuclear family units as the starting base.

Yet whilst the event should be relationship-based, there can be an appropriate place for a clear, simple, all-age friendly presentation of the good news within them. It may occasionally be possible for this to be in the form of an all-age talk involving visuals and participation. But it might also be through testimony, interviews, drama, poetry, video, magic tricks which illustrate the good news, escapology, puppets, juggling or dance. It is not the place of this book to outline exactly how such methods can be used but be assured they are all possible and suitable.

Some obviously rely on the skills of an artiste, others may be home-grown. There is value in bringing someone from outside to present the good news in whatever form is chosen, but make sure that they are good and are going to present the gospel, not simply entertain. Brief any such visitors well. They need to know about the context, venue, nature of 'audience', that it is for 'families' not simply a specific age group, how long they have, what they will be paid (the labourer is worthy of her hire), how to find the place, what facilities are available, what follow-up is planned and about the prayer that is going into the event.

Any such events must be well-planned, thoroughly prayed for, and run to the highest possible standards. You may not see many people make conscious decisions to follow Christ, but they could do – and for many these events may well be key points in the long journey to faith.

Day Events
Some of the ideas described already would work as day events. The workshop format clearly lends itself to the possibility of lasting for half a day, or even a whole one. A treasure hunt could actually be quite a major event lasting several hours. Another possibility for a half or whole day is to run some kind of 'family' sports event or an all-age 'It's a Knockout'. Linking these with the testimony of a Christian sports personality (preferably live or alternatively on video) can work well. A 'day event' might also be simply a day out for a group of families with almost nothing planned other than the date, destination and food. The aim would be to build friendships and extend the principle of family to family in a wider grouping.

A Whole Weekend
A whole weekend geared around families doing things together is also possible. Everyone stays in their own home

as normal, but meets together with other 'family groups' for a whole series of events through the weekend. These could include:

> a swimming session in the local pool
> using a number of courts for different activities in a local sports centre or park
> breakfast in 'family groups' with an activity to do
> family workshops
> some creative Bible exploration in 'family groups'
> a barn dance on the Saturday evening
> a family film and a meal together.

Be creative with such a weekend. Allow people to drop in and out of the various activities, but have a common thread running through them all. The more people join in, the more they will understand of the good news which is being communicated through the overall experience of the weekend. In an evangelistic context weekends like these ought to pick up a theme which relates to the needs of the families involved. Themes of 'peace' or 'hope' or 'caring for our world' are likely to make more sense and connect with people's worlds better than 'the case for the resurrection'. The activities and materials must allow for plenty of interaction and reflection on real family life situations, to see what difference the good news makes to them. It is not about *making* the gospel relevant, but about demonstrating that it *is* relevant because of the way it affects real life.

Conclusions

It is all too easy to plan and run 'one off' events like those suggested above and then think that you have 'done' family evangelism. This is a long way from the truth. These events can only truly be described as part of any process of reaching families when they are planned and run by a church in the much broader context of ongoing involvement with the community. We can only honestly regard ourselves as being in the business of reaching families when we are seeking to be God's 'good news family community' within our locality. As such we should be concerned with the broadest needs of families and constantly seeking to meet these in a long-term consistent way. When we do this, 'one off' events actually cease to be that; they are just another part of the overall picture. When used in this way they are likely to be more valuable, better attended and have a clearer role in our overall concern to reach families with the gospel.

> ### Stop
>
> Consider any 'one off' events you have been involved in.
>
> - What were the good and weak points about them?
> - Consider one of the ideas in this chapter which may be new to you. What do you make of the idea?
> - How far do any 'one off' events you have already run actually fit into an overall strategy? What needs to be done to improve this?

Resources

The Bumper Book of Family Activities, John Marshall, Scripture Union, 1994.

Family Evangelism, John Hattam, Scripture Union Missions Department, (see page 106).

12

THE GOSPEL THAT DIVIDES?

Jesus said, 'I tell you... anyone who leaves home or brothers or sisters or mother or father or children or fields for me and for the gospel, will receive... a hundred times more...' (Mark 10:29, 30).

When Jesus' mother and brothers came to see him and speak with him, he said, 'Who is my mother? Who are my brothers?' He looked at the people sitting round him and said, 'Look! Here are my mother and my brothers! Whoever does what God wants him to do is my brother, my sister, my mother' (Mark 3:33–35).

Jesus warned his followers, 'Men will hand over their own brothers to be put to death, and fathers will do the same to their children. Children will turn against their parents and have them put to death' (Mark 13:12, GNB). This is the very opposite of the promise for the messianic age (Malachi 4:5–6, Luke 1:17). Jesus not only speaks of this happening at the end of the age; he also warned his disciples about it when he sent them out to the villages of Israel (Matthew 10:21).

> Do not think that I have come to bring peace to the world. No, I did not come to bring peace, but a sword. I came to set sons against their fathers, daughters against their mothers, daughters-in-law against their mothers-in-law; your worst enemies will be the members of your own family.

> Those who love their father or mother more than me are not fit to be my disciples; those who love their son or daughter more than me are not fit to be my disciples. Those who do not take up their cross and follow in my footsteps are not fit to be my disciples.
> (*Matthew 10:34–38*)

These are remarkable words from the Lord himself. Following him will cause the division of families. Loyalty to Jesus and the rule of God must come higher than loyalty to our kin and blood relatives, even those closest to us.

Yet these words were spoken by the one who lived as a faithful son for thirty years; whose last words were for his mother and her welfare; who lambasted the legal experts for the way they twisted the law to avoid fulfilling their family obligations; who endorsed the marriage relationship as God's idea and intention for most human beings even within his kingdom. What is it about? Why are these words so carefully preserved and included in the Gospel writers' texts? If they had wanted to create a neat picture of Jesus as loyal family man, they would surely have left out these words. But they keep them in and even give them some prominence.

These words were kept in because they were of great importance to the first readers of the Gospels. Here were people scattered around the Roman Empire who had committed their lives to following Jesus as the crucified and risen Saviour. They believed he had rescued them from the coming judgement and that they would be with him forever. They had turned their backs either on their Jewish or their pagan faith. Now many of them were being disowned by their families and facing persecution. Their own family members were turning on them and handing them over to the Roman authorities for imprisonment, torture and death. What kind of reward was that for following

Jesus? Perhaps they had been wrong about him. Perhaps they should give up this new 'Way' and return to their Jewish or pagan roots.

Into such situations, these words of Jesus must have spoken powerfully. The persecution they were facing wasn't evidence that they were wrong or that Jesus had abandoned them; in fact it was evidence that they were being true to him. Now they had to stand fast and not give up in the face of suffering, even if it came from their own blood relatives. He would provide alternative family support, not through the family of blood, but the family of faith. Peter's first letter could almost be seen as a commentary on these Gospel verses.

Notice that the only action 'against' the kinship family commended by Jesus is the commitment to follow him and serve in God's kingdom. Such a decision, made clear by his own life and words, is not an excuse to abandon family responsibilities. Jesus' followers are to ensure that their families' needs are provided for. They should hold fast to the fourth commandment and honour their parents whatever age they might be. But their highest priority will be to follow Christ.

This ongoing commitment to the kinship family is expressed time and again in the epistles (1 Timothy 3, Titus 1:6; Ephesians 6:1–3; Colossians 3:20; Ephesians 5:22ff; Colossians 3:18–19; 1 Timothy 3:2; 12; Titus 1:6; Hebrews 13:4; 1 Corinthians 7; 1 Peter 3:1ff).

As we reach out to families, part of our calling is to teach those who choose to follow Christ that it involves a commitment to loving and caring for the kinship family, whether or not other members of that family choose to follow Christ themselves.

However, the warning is clear: the decision to take Jesus as Lord of one's life and to seek above all else God's rule and justice may cause division within the family as members of the family reject a believer because of that decision. A Christian cannot turn round to their parents or husband or wife and say, 'I can no longer live with you because I am following Jesus now', but the non-believer might choose to throw them out. The believer is to do all in their power to live at peace with their family; to care for them; to provide for them; to live a life which expresses the life of Christ to them. If, however, people 'love darkness rather than light', there may come a point of rejection and even outright opposition. It must only be on the basis of rejecting goodness though, and not because of wrong behaviour by the Christian (1 Peter 3:13–22).

> **Stop**
>
> How do you feel about all of this? What are your gut reactions and concerns? What do you think might be some of the practical outcomes of it all?

Practical Possibilities

It is impossible to predict how people will react to the good news as it begins to make an impact on their family life. As we seek to share it with families rather than simply with individuals in families, we must accept that different individuals will react to it and receive it in different ways.

Our prayer and desire must be to see all members of family households responding positively to Jesus. Our longing must be for the wholeness of the household and this will include seeing the whole household expressing faith and commitment to Jesus. Yet it is likely to be very rare in modern Western societies that all members of a household will find faith at the same time. Western society is markedly different from that of the Philippian jailer, or from many two-thirds world communities where family solidarity and acting as one remain the norm.

The words of the New Testament epistles may suddenly take on a whole new relevance as a wife or husband consider what it means to follow Christ whilst married to a partner who does not yet share that commitment. Children will have to think through carefully what honouring their parents means in practice, whether those parents be elderly and frail, or young, spritely and in no apparent need of caring support. Honouring parents changes with the age, ability and circumstances of both the child and the parent. It is never static, but rather an ever-moving, developing relationship between maturing human beings.

The church family must welcome the new faith and commitment of the one family member without rejecting the other(s). There should be no sense of pushing away those who have as yet chosen not to believe. It is remarkably easy to give this impression by our actions, words or both. The 'not-yet believer' will not be won over by a newly trenchant relative or over-zealous friends; they will be won over by the evidence of Christ's spirit in their relative's life and in the lives of the Christian community to which that relative now belongs. Such a process may take years or it may never happen. Care needs to be taken to help the new believer avoid suddenly being out at church meetings every night and losing touch with the people at home. Thought has to be given to how that person might take part in the worship and life of the kingdom, without needlessly alienating the remainder of the family. Too often mistakes have been made in this way. Zeal and good intention are usually wonderful, but the lack of thought and the negative impact can be very damaging.

So our desire and work will always be to see the rule of God coming into every part of each family's life. There should be no desire to break up a family, pull a member away from a family, or suggest lack of love for the family.

And this must be true, whatever the background of the people involved. Someone from a Muslim family background coming to faith in Jesus should seek to love and care for all their family members, and be given all the support they may need to do so. Their family may choose to reject them, but rejection and division should never arise from the Christian side, though historically and sadly this has often happened. And while most people in Western society will come to faith in Christ from a secular humanist background, they may equally find themselves rejected.

There is certainly no place for targeting families for our evangelistic efforts from other major world faiths. They are neighbours alongside all our other neighbours; they are part of the wider community just as those from no faith background. They all have an equal right to be loved by us with the love of God revealed in Christ. 'Love your neighbour as yourself' must mean wanting the best for all our neighbours.

When rejection does occur and division is created within a family, then the family of God's people clearly ought to become the alternative family for the one rejected. A new home may be needed. Friendship and support will be vital. Too easily when the chips are really down, such people find themselves lacking the real family support that they need.

Conclusions

There will be occasions when the good news of God's reconciling love, universal justice and dynamic peace will actually bring division. This happens not because it is God's deepest desire or the desire of his followers, but because people will choose 'darkness rather than light' and reject grace rather than receive it. Their choice will show itself on occasions by outright hostility. The gospel can divide families.

Yet this gospel is intended to bring about reconciliation,

not only between God and people, but also between people and people. It is intended to be good news for people in their family contexts. Whilst it creates a whole new family in which all who follow Christ are equally children of the one heavenly Father, God longs that all members of human families are incorporated into his family. It must grieve him as it should grieve his people that they are not.

Stop

In what ways might the life of your local church be creating unnecessary division in households? What could be done to change this?

13

FAMILIES OF THE FUTURE

The vision of reaching family households together with the good news of God is, I am convinced, a right one. It fits with the nature of God, the nature of being human and the need for community, the lack of which is felt deeply throughout the disaffected, isolated, alienated and tired Western world.

It is a vision which offers immense flexibility. This is because it is not a vision of a new methodology for evangelism, but of a community committed to relationship: between God and his created order; between God and human beings made in the divine image; between people connected by blood, covenant, neighbourhood and common humanity. Relationships are always dynamic. The only static relationships are those maintained between two dead people. You cannot be alive and have a static relationship with anyone or anything. That is why this vision cannot be of a methodology. Methods have a habit of being tightly defined and held in a static mode. Relationships simply do not fit methods. It is therefore a vision which can find its expression in a host of ways, not in a particular set of formulae. It will serve us well in a world which is changing so rapidly that no one can keep up, a world desperately seeking new meaning and purpose, and hope as it enters into a new millenium.

Family patterns have changed enormously over the past

few decades. The apparently settled norms of the nuclear family have been blown away and no amount of talking about getting back to basic family values will actually halt the shifting patterns of 'family' which have occurred and will continue into the next generation. We do well to remind ourselves that there never was any settled norm. It was a pattern which held sway for a relatively long period in modern history, but it never was the pattern of the ancient world, nor that of medieval or even Renaissance Western life. The shift we are going through now apparently does have some new features, most notably the growth in families without fathers living in them. But the fact of changes in family patterns is not a new phenomenon. History tells us that the family as a unit did not fall apart in previous shifts; indeed it has proved utterly resilient. It may well be that it will prove just as resilient once again. Take, as an example, the following observation written by Barbara Ehrenreich (*The Guardian*, 11 June 1994):

> I asked myself, as I do every year in this season of graduations and weddings: why does divorce not destroy the family, as promised? Why does the family just keep on expanding? That was the idea, you will recall, propounded by legions of chin-stroking commentators: that divorce would reduce the family to rubble and rend the 'very fabric of society', leaving us all to live like reptiles, bereft of the comfort of kin, every man for himself. Divorce, we were told, was a calamity which would produce a generation of bedwetters, not to mention all the embittered, alcoholic, ex-spouses. But, contrary to expectation, divorce has itself become part of the 'fabric of society' – binding us together in vast multicultural alliances from which there is, alas, no legal or moral escape.

Families of the future

It wouldn't be right for biblical Christians to look back to the Bible for alternative models of being family simply in order to recreate them. Undoubtedly our hearts and minds will cry out for the broader based, more fully inclusive, extended families seen in Bible times. But these were families in a different world and in different cultures. We cannot recreate them as we enter the twenty-first century. We will need to find and develop new ways of being 'family'. These ways will include the divinely given gift of marriage; they will reflect the reality of the divine family image; and they will incorporate the reality that the Lord of all creation was complete as a human being without being married or fathering children. But exactly what shape these families may take is impossible to predict.

Our calling is not to try and hold on conservatively to a supposedly Christian model of family life, in the face of all the changes in our society. It will rather be to demonstrate radically new alternatives which reflect the life and purpose of God, in contrast to the models based only on the belief in human selfhood. This modelling will be within family households, however they may turn out to be constituted. And it will be seen in all God's people as they live out what it means to be the community of God's kingdom, established by him to declare his love and grace to the world.

As this 'family' life of God is demonstrated by the followers of Jesus, families, and the individuals within them, will be reached with the good news that this God is for them through the overflowing, outward-looking relationships of God's people together. It will happen in every area of life related to being family: the care of the elderly and lonely; the welcoming of the stranger and the needy; the raising of children, in a way which embraces their physical, mental, emotional, moral and spiritual welfare. It will reach out to young and old alike; to families of all shapes and sizes. And as the love and power of God – revealed in and through the life, dying and rising of Jesus of Nazareth – is demonstrated and shared with families around us, so they will be changed, not into nice, neat nuclear Christian households, but rather into radical, open mini-communities of faith linked with similar households offering the alternative kingdom which is the kingdom of God.

Perhaps it all sounds too good to be true; a vision but not a reality. Maybe. But without vision we perish. We will settle for the mediocre and the mediocre cannot possibly be God's desire. We need to hold the vision before us and begin to work towards its realisation. This will mean much prayer on the part of individuals, families, local church communities, groups of such local church communities together and wider based bodies. Prayer will be at the heart of the vision. It will also be at the heart of reaching families for Christ. We must pray for the Holy Spirit to enable and empower us and to open the eyes of families around to the truth and reality of God's love.

There must also be a willingness to examine afresh the lives of Christians in families and the corporate life of local church communities. Changes will have to be made so that each is regarded far more as a community of the King. Then, these communities will need to recognise and accept others in their locality openly, to work and pray together. In households, local church fellowships and groups of fellowships the people of God should be regarded as people through whom the triune God longs to express his life to the lost world around them. It is a call to a different way of being church.

Alongside this will be practical activities which will seek to express God's love to family households. These will be done not as 'one off' events so that 'family evangelism' can be ticked off on a list of 'evangelistic things we ought to do', but rather in a way which is strategically planned and designed to meet the needs of the community in which a local church is set. These activities should enhance the

Families of the future

communication of the good news through developing relationships on a long term basis rather than as hit and run evangelistic events.

In seeking to reach families we will be committing ourselves to the long haul not the short sharp burst. Such commitment will be costly. Those who follow Christ can expect the same treatment as Christ: hailed as wonderful when the miracles occur; listened to with fascination when the stories are told; admired for the authority, humility and goodness of his life; but slandered and sneered at, rejected and reviled when he insisted on putting God, his rule and justice first. As we seek to reach families, it will not always be a success; but it will always be glorious because we will be doing the Father's will.